Walt Whitman's Western Jaunt

WALTER H. EITNER

THE REGENTS PRESS OF KANSAS
Lawrence

Illustrations were obtained from the following sources, and are used here by permission: (1) 1880 portrait from the Collection of American Literature, Beinecke Rare Book and Manuscript Library, Yale University; (2, 3, 4) Historical Society of Pennsylvania; (5) from H. B. Binns, *A Life of Walt Whitman*, London, 1905; (6, 21, 22, 23) Missouri Historical Society; (7, 8, 9, 10, 11, 12, 13, 14) Kansas State Historical Society; (15, 16, 18) Denver Public Library, Western History Department; (17) Colorado Historical Society; (19, 20) Kansas City Public Library.

Library of Congress Cataloging in Publication Data

Eitner, Walter H   1919-
Walt Whitman's Western jaunt.

Bibliography: p.
Includes index.
1. Whitman, Walt, 1819-1892—Journeys—The West.
2. Poets, American—19th century—Biography.
3. The West—Description and travel—1860-1880.
4. The West in literature. I. Title.
PS3234.E34   811'.3   [B]   80-29336
ISBN 0-7006-0212-7

TO

IRENE

Contents

List of Illustrations

Maps

Preface

Walt Whitman's 1879 trip to the West—first to Kansas, then on to Denver and the Rockies—was made late in his life, when he was sixty, after most of his truly creative work had been accomplished. During the seventies he had published *Democratic Vistas* (1871) and the fifth edition of *Leaves of Grass* (1871–72). Early in 1873 he had had a paralytic stroke, and that year (the same year in which his mother died) he had moved from Washington, D.C., to his brother George's house in Camden, New Jersey, the city that was to be his permanent address for the rest of his life. There he had managed to bring out a special issue (the Author's Edition) of *Leaves of Grass* to mark the nation's centennial. He had had no role, however, in the ceremonies of the International Exhibition, the centennial celebration at neighboring Philadelphia. As Robert Scholnick demonstrates, that year a British-American debate, generated by Whitman himself, on whether he was a persecuted poet, had brought him a flurry of publicity that helped sell the commemorative issue and led to the widening of his readership.[1] By the time he headed for Kansas, though he was far from being the people's poet that, say, Whittier was, he was not without recognition in his own country.

By 1879, though Whitman's main poetic statements had been made, his writing career was far from over. A year after the trip he would bring out the sixth edition of *Leaves of Grass* (1881), in which he would give his poems their final arrangement. *Specimen Days* and *Collect* would come out in 1882, *November Boughs* in 1888, *Goodbye My Fancy* in 1891, and the so-called Deathbed Edition of *Leaves of Grass* in 1891–92.

The western jaunt yielded very little poetry, though it confirmed ("tallied with"), Whitman thought, the ideas and images of the West he had earlier presented in *Leaves of Grass*. Only four poems in the 1881 edition may be assigned specifically to the trip: "Italian Music in Dakota," "The

Prairie States," "Spirit That Form'd This Scene," and "What Best I See in Thee" (written in St. Louis). "A Prairie Sunset" (1888) is a later recollection.

Whitman, of course, describes his trip in *Specimen Days*. It has been studied in detail by Robert R. Hubach in his Indiana University dissertation, "Walt Whitman and the West" (1943). A brief account is in Gay Wilson Allen's *Solitary Singer* (1955). What I attempt in this new study is a thorough review of the trip in the light of more recent scholarship. With the publication of Whitman's daybooks and notebooks now supplementing his collected correspondence, and with a definitive and annotative edition of *Specimen Days* available, a further inquiry seems justified.

We can now reconstruct much of Whitman's western experience, including a fairly well-detailed itinerary, and compare it with his account in *Specimen Days*. This study in part constitutes a criticism of the sections of that book dealing with the West by examining the ways in which Whitman reordered his experiences to have them support a bardic pose he wished to maintain. It also shows him very much his own press agent, writing his own interviews, and sending back to the press in the East promotional accounts of his whereabouts, his health, and his plans. To demonstrate the extent of these matters I risk repetitiveness in relying on numerous, sometimes similar, quotations.

One omission in *Specimen Days* that is left mainly unrepaired in earlier studies is Whitman's failure to report his traveling companions. Both Hubach and Allen note that Whitman traveled with the Philadelphia publisher John W. Forney; and Hubach quotes newspaper items containing the names of Whitman's other fellow-travelers: J. M. W. Geist, E. K. Martin, and W. W. Reitzel. But that is all. What makes Whitman's companions important and deserving of further attention here is the fact that, except for Reitzel, they were all correspondents for Pennsylvania newspapers, and their reports of the trip (and of the poet) are rewarding. In this study I fully restore them to the record.

Acknowledgments

For assistance with this work I am grateful for the support of the Faculty Research Award Committee, the Graduate School, Kansas State University; for the benefit of a semester's sabbatical leave granted by the College of Arts and Sciences; and for other released time and funding by the Department of English.

I also wish to express my thanks to the librarians and their assistants at Farrell Library, Kansas State University; and to the staffs of these other libraries and institutions: American Heritage Center, University of Wyoming, Laramie; Camden County Historical Society, Camden, New Jersey; Champaign County Library, Urbana, Ohio; Colorado Historical Society, Denver; Denver Public Library; Free Library of Philadelphia; the Ft. Riley Cavalry Museum, Ft. Riley, Kansas; Historical Society of Pennsylvania, Philadelphia; Kansas City Public Library, Kansas City, Missouri; Kansas State Historical Society, Topeka; Lancaster County Library, Lancaster, Pennsylvania; Library Company of Philadelphia; Manhattan Public Library, Manhattan, Kansas; Missouri Historical Society, St. Louis; Princeton University Library; Watson Library and Spencer Research Library, the University of Kansas, Lawrence; St. Louis Mercantile Library Association; St. Louis Public Library; Van Pelt Library, the University of Pennsylvania.

Portions of this work appeared in somewhat different form in the following publications, and are used here by permission: "Walt Whitman's Companions Report His Western Trip," *The Markham Review* (Fall 1980); "Whitman's *Daybooks*: Further Identifications," *Walt Whitman Review* (June 1980); "Some Further Autograph Notes of Whitman's 1879 Western Trip," *Walt Whitman Review* (March 1980); and "Walt Whitman and the Kansas Silver Wedding," *Kanhistique* (September 1979).

I am indebted to the New York University Press for a broad freedom to quote from the *Collected Writings of Walt Whitman*; to the Princeton University Library for permission to quote from Rollins, "Walt Whitman, Autograph notes . . . ," in the Western Americana Collections there; and to the American Heritage Center, University of Wyoming, for the use of a quotation from the diaries of Leonard Eicholtz.

Chronology & Itinerary

The five travelers departed on 10 September 1879. Although his traveling companions returned to the East earlier, Whitman was not back in Camden until 5 January 1880. See the route of their travels on map 1 (page 16).

Wednesday, 10 September 1879. Whitman departs 431 Stevens Street, Camden, New Jersey. Takes ferry to Market Street, Philadelphia. Departs (with Forney, Martin, and Reitzel) from West Philadelphia Station, 9:10 P.M., Pennsylvania Railroad. Geist boards the train at Lancaster.

Thursday, 11 September. Breakfast at Pittsburgh, Pennsylvania. The party changes to the Pan Handle Railroad. Delayed by train accident at Urbana, Ohio.

Friday, 12 September. Party arrives at St. Louis early in the morning. Breakfast at the Planters' Hotel. Tours the city. That night Whitman stays at brother's house, 2316 Pine Street. The others stay at the Planters' Hotel.

Saturday, 13 September. Party departs St. Louis 9:00 A.M. via the St. Louis, Kansas City and Northern Railway. Arrives late that night at Kansas City, Missouri. Met by Old Settlers' committee and escorted via Kansas Pacific Railway to Lawrence, Kansas.

Sunday, 14 September. Whitman a guest (with Forney) in home of John P. Usher, mayor of Lawrence. Tours Lawrence and the University of Kansas campus.

Monday, 15 September. Attends Old Settlers' meeting at Bismarck Grove, outside Lawrence. Hears Forney and Edward Everett Hale, guest speakers.

Tuesday, 16 September. Whitman fails to attend the Old Settlers' second session. Visits with Usher's sons. Group departs in the evening via Kansas Pacific for Topeka, Kansas. Arrives there around 8:30 P.M., and is escorted to the Tefft House.

Wednesday, 17 September. Party visits the state capitol. Tours Topeka.

Thursday, 18 September. Meets a group of Indians. Farewell banquet at the Palace Hotel. The travelers (without Forney) depart around 3 P.M. westward via the Kansas Pacific. Supper at Abilene, Kansas.

Friday, 19 September. Breakfast at Wallace, Kansas. Dinner at Hugo, Colorado. The group arrives in Denver at 4:30 P.M. Stays at the American House.

Saturday, 20 September. Geist and Martin go to Leadville, Colorado. Reitzel and Whitman visit Denver.

Sunday, 21 September. In Denver.

Monday, 22 September. Reitzel and Whitman take early morning train of the Denver, South Park and Pacific Railroad. Travel via Platte Canyon and Kenosha Pass to meet Geist and Martin at Red Hill in South Park. The four go to the end of the track at Garos. Arrive back in Denver around 10:00 P.M.

Tuesday, 23 September. The travelers depart Denver at 8:00 A.M. via the Denver and Rio Grande Railway. At Pueblo they transfer to the Atchison, Topeka and Santa Fe.

Wednesday, 24 September. They arrive in Sterling, Kansas. Whitman visits Civil War friend, Ed Lindsey. Geist and Martin attend a Republican meeting.

Thursday, 25 September. They depart Sterling on 4:50 A.M. train. Arrive in Kansas City around 6:00 P.M. Stay at the Coates House.

Friday, 26 September. Group visits Kansas City, including the Industrial and Agricultural Exhibition. Departs Kansas City in the evening.

Saturday, 27 September. The party arrives in St. Louis in the morning. Whitman goes to his brother's house. The others continue eastward, and arrive home in Pennsylvania the evening of the twenty-eighth.

Whitman stays in St. Louis until the new year. Between spells of illness he visits the city and the area. Works at his book business.

Sunday, 4 January 1880. Whitman departs St. Louis 8:00 A.M.

Monday, 5 January. Arrives West Philadelphia 7:20 P.M. Home in Camden shortly thereafter.

1

The argument for travelling abroad is not all on one side. There are pulses of irresistible ardor, with due reasons why they may not be gainsaid. But a calm man of deep vision will find, in this tremendous modern spectacle of America, at least as great sights as anything the foreign world, or the antique, or the relics of the antique, can afford him. Why shall I travel to Rome to see the old pillars of the Forum, only important for those who lived there ages ago? Shall I journey four thousand miles to weigh the ashes of some corpses? Shall I not vivify myself with life here, rushing, tumultous [sic], scornful, masterful, oceanic—greater than ever before known?

"A Christmas Garland, in Prose and Verse," 1874

1

The Five Travelers

In the fall of 1879 Walt Whitman made a widely publicized trip to the West—first, to Kansas for the Old Settlers' Quarter Centennial celebration near Lawrence, then on to Denver and the Rockies. It was his first trip beyond the Mississippi valley, though he had, over thirty years before, gone down the Ohio and Mississippi rivers to a briefly held newspaper job in New Orleans. That earlier jaunt, with his brother Thomas Jefferson ("Jeff"), included visits to St. Louis, Milwaukee, and Chicago, and helped him gather, Whitman believed, the "main part" of the "physiology" of *Leaves of Grass*.[1] The new journey, then, was to take him even farther into a West he had already recorded in the imagery of five editions of *Leaves of Grass* and in *Democratic Vistas*. And now he was sixty and walking with a cane, a "half-Paralytic" from the effects of a stroke six years earlier.[2]

Whitman's record of the 1879 jaunt is open to us in numerous daybook notes and in other jottings, in a few extant letters, and, extensively, in several sections of *Specimen Days* (1882). It is, however, even with Whitman's private notes now largely available, a sketchily and to a certain extent an inaccurately presented report. Whitman omitted much, and pretended much. Like many other travelers, in the reciting he made what he wanted to out of his journey, even at the risk of falsehood.

A measure of the difference between the fact and the fiction of the account of the trip in *Specimen Days* can be drawn at the outset from considering the point of view Whitman uses there. Although he frequently employs the first person plural, he never directly states that he is traveling in company, as in fact he is. Since his pronoun suggests the "editorial we," he leaves the impression that he is traveling alone, thereby making the journey appear more adventurous, himself more romantic.

In only one brief passage is there a suggestion, a veiled one, that he is in company. In the section "Missouri State" he reports the "rolling prairies" as "agriculturally perfect view'd from Pennsylvania and New Jersey eyes."[3] The New Jersey eyes are presumably his own, for by this time he had lived over six years in his brother George's house in Camden. The Pennsylvania eyes would be those of John W. Forney, the editor and publisher of a Philadelphia weekly, *Progress*; William W. Reitzel, the business manager of *Progress;* J. M. W. Geist, the editor of the *Lancaster* (Pennsylvania) *Daily New Era*; and E. K. Martin, a correspondent for the *Philadelphia Press*. All four of Whitman's companions, though Forney and Reitzel were living in Philadelphia, were Lancasterians. With the rich agricultural area of Lancaster County in their backgrounds, they probably had discerning eyes for judging the Missouri land passing by their train windows.

On 19 July 1879, John W. Forney reported in *Progress* that he had accepted an invitation from the Old Settlers of Kansas to speak at their celebration of twenty-five years of settlement (dating from when the territory of Kansas was organized).[4] The Silver Wedding, as it was called, was to be held on 15 and 16 September at Bismarck Grove, a rustic convention center just outside Lawrence. When Forney accepted, the Kansans gained a speaker who, at sixty-two, was in the later years of a nationally prominent career in journalism and public affairs. He had been secretary of the U.S. Senate and clerk of the U.S. House of Representatives, and had presided over the latter body during the two months, 2 December 1855 to 2 February 1856, when it struggled through 133 ballots to choose a Speaker of the House—finally electing a Free Soiler, Nathaniel P. Banks of Massachusetts. As editor of two influential newspapers, the *Philadelphia Pennsylvanian* and the *Wash-*

2. John W. Forney, editor and publisher, *Progress*

ington Daily Union, Forney had been an important figure in the
Democratic party and a strong supporter of James Buchanan.[5]

Forney was remembered best by the Kansans, however, for his
break with Buchanan, which came about, among other reasons, over
the president's recommendation that Kansas be admitted as a state
under the proslavery Lecompton constitution. Forney then turned Republican, and later, during the Civil War, closely supported Lincoln.
He became the leading war-time Republican editor of papers in Philadelphia and Washington. His *Philadelphia Press* was distributed
among the Union Army, and his *Washington Chronicle* came close to
being an organ of the Lincoln administration.[6]

The Old Settlers, then, were calling on a man they remembered as a Free Soil advocate. "I hope you can attend and represent the old-time Anti-Lecompton Democracy. That Spartan band should have its champion at the celebration," George A. Crawford had written for the invitations committee.[7] Forney in turn asked three other old Free Soilers to go along: Nathaniel P. Banks, Walt Whitman, and J. M. W. Geist. His long-time congressional friend, Banks, sent his regrets that he could not get away.[8] Whitman, however, "embraced the opportunity," seeing the trip as a chance to visit Jeff and his two nieces, Mannahatta ("Hattie") and Jessie, in St. Louis, where his brother was the water commissioner, and, possibly, to see more of the West by going on to Denver.[9]

3. J. M. W. Geist, editor, *Lancaster Daily New Era*

6

Forney and Whitman had been together frequently that summer, and *Progress* had been giving the poet some attention.[10] In August it reprinted his poem, "O Captain! My Captain!"[11] Earlier, in the same issue in which he announced his trip to Kansas, Forney noted that Whitman was at home in Camden, and "as fresh and sound as a Newtown pippin in a snow wreath."[12]

In fact, that same day, 19 July, the two men had participated in a shipboard send-off ceremony for Thomas M. Coleman ("Nameloc"), city editor of the *Philadelphia Public Ledger*, bound for a European vacation. On that occasion twenty-three of Coleman's colleagues and friends boarded his ship at Philadelphia that morning to accompany him down the Delaware. When the ship was near Gloucester they gathered "on the after-saloon deck beside the wheel-house" for a farewell ceremony, for which Whitman was unanimously elected to preside. As the chairman it may have been Whitman who, first, read a letter of regret from Governor Henry M. Hoyt saying that he was unable to attend, and who then introduced a series of farewell speakers, including Forney. The latter turned first to Whitman as "Mr. President," and told him: "You are appropriately where you are now on your pedestal, because you, Walt Whitman, as a born printer, and with all respect, are entitled to our special regards, and are in an appropriate place today among your friends—sincere friends—who are as glad to see you as they are sorry to bid goodbye to Mr. Coleman."[13] The celebrants finally said goodbye to Coleman off Chester, where they transferred to a police steam tug for the return trip.[14]

Geist and Whitman were probably well acquainted through Forney. On one occasion, at least, they had been together that summer, for Geist had also attended the Coleman send-off, and had reported it, including Whitman's participation and Forney's remarks, in his paper.[15]

Geist and Forney had known each other since their early days in Lancaster, and Geist at one time had been news editor on Forney's *Pennsylvanian*. After varied service on a number of newspapers in the state, he had gone back to Lancaster to be editor of the *Saturday Evening Express*. In that position he had opposed the extension of slavery into Kansas, supported the election of Banks as Speaker, and in 1856 helped found the Republican party in Lancaster County.[16]

In going on the trip to Kansas, Geist was, at fifty-four, taking a needed vacation, his first, as he explained to his *Daily New Era* readers, since April 1877 when he and ex-State Senator John B. Warfel founded the paper.[17] He must have carried some worries away with him, however, for on his return he and Warfel would have to face trial in a libel suit which had been brought against them that summer for publishing a story involving their county solicitor and the district attorney in an alleged political payoff.[18]

At thirty-four, E. K. Martin was the youngest of the group, and the only one of them who had seen service as a combatant in the Civil War. He had dropped out of Phillips Academy in Andover, Massachusetts, to enlist, at sixteen, in the Lancaster County Regiment. He had fought under Buell in the strategically important battle of Perryville, Kentucky. Subsequently, he had served under Rosecrans and Thomas, and had been with Sherman in the "march to the sea." After the war he completed his studies at Phillips, and went on to Amherst College, graduating in 1871. He then studied law at Columbia, and in 1876 was admitted to the bar in Lancaster County.[19] Like Forney, he was an able speaker. Two years before the trip he had delivered the main address at the first reunion of his regiment, held on the fifteenth anniversary of the Perryville battle, their "baptism of fire." His speech was published as a pamphlet by Geist, and with his friend's prefacing note.[20]

Martin did some occasional writing for the *Daily New Era*, and sometimes advised its proprietors in legal matters. He was, in fact, slated to appear as a defense witness in their libel case.[21] Just before the trip, Martin had gotten out of some legal difficulties of his own. For calling the district attorney (the same official Geist was entangled with) a "liar" in front of a judge, he had been fined ten dollars for contempt of court. Geist had given him good publicity in the matter, making much of Martin's "manly" deportment in what became a defense of his reputation.[22]

Either Geist or Forney may have suggested adding Martin to the party. As a Republican he was a kindred spirit. Forney had recently

8

4. E. K. Martin, correspondent for the *Philadelphia Press*

published in *Progress* Martin's article on "Lancaster County Politics,"[23] and he may have helped arrange for him to travel as correspondent for the *Press*, a paper Forney had sold only two years before.[24]

The "fifth wheel," as Geist called him, was William W. Reitzel, Forney's brother-in-law as well as business manager. "But in this case," Geist wrote,

> we found our *fifth* the most useful . . . the *cicerone* of the party. Having been for many years connected in a responsible position with the Adams Express Company, travelling West and South, he was thoroughly familiar with all the details of railroading, and

under his vigilant eye never a satchel, overcoat or parcel was in danger of being overlooked or of getting astray. Quiet in demeanor, genial in manner, overflowing with good humor, and withal a strict teetotaller, without parading his abstinence as a merit, he was the favorite of every circle of new acquaintances formed on the route.[25]

These are the men Whitman traveled with on the 1879 journey. It is remarkable that he does not mention them in the western sections of *Specimen Days* (which otherwise has individual identifications by names or initials). For over two weeks they lived closely and traveled far together—as comrades, even, on the open road.

2

In a few years the dominion-heart of America will be far inland, toward the West. Our future national capital may not be where the present one is. It is possible, nay likely, that in less than fifty years, it will migrate a thousand or two miles, will be refounded, and every thing belonging to it made on a different plan, original, far more superb. The main social, political, spine-character of the States will probably run along the Ohio, Missouri and Mississippi rivers, and west and north of them, including Canada. Those regions, with the group of powerful brothers toward the Pacific, (destined to the mastership of that sea and its countless paradises of islands,) will compact and settle the traits of America, with all the old retain'd, but more expanded, grafted on newer, hardier, purely native stock. A giant growth, composite from the rest, getting their contribution, absorbing it, to make it more illustrious. From the north, intellect, the sun of things, also the idea of unswayable justice, anchor amid the last, the wildest tempests. From the south the living soul, the animus of good and bad, haughtily admitting no demonstration but its own. While from the west itself comes solid personality, with blood and brawn, and the deep quality of all-accepting fusion.

Democratic Vistas, 1871

From Camden to Lawrence

Sometime on Wednesday, 10 September 1879, Whitman left his third-floor room in his brother's house at 431 Stevens Street in Camden, New Jersey, and headed for the rail depot in West Philadelphia. He had been living with George and his wife, Louisa ("Lou"), since 1873, following his stroke in Washington, D.C.

We have to imagine his setting out. He probably took a horsecar to the Federal Street ferry. There, using a pass, he made the brief crossing over the Delaware River to Philadelphia.[1] It was a clear day, pleasantly cool with light winds from the north—a good day for beginning a journey.[2]

Arriving at Market Street (near where young Ben Franklin had first arrived in Philadelphia over a hundred years earlier), Whitman again used a streetcar to get to the Pennsylvania Railroad depot at Thirty-second and Market. There, if he hadn't met them along the way—at the *Progress* office, or perhaps at Guy's Hotel—he joined up with Forney, Reitzel, and Martin to board the Cincinnati Express.

This trek out to the railroad station was over very familiar territory. The ferry crossing Whitman had made many times, and he was well acquainted with the captains and crews. And Philadelphia, lying as a "vast, firm chessboard" in its "unmeasurable spread of little squares," as another sixty-year-old, Henry James, was to describe it twenty-five years later,[3] was a place of comfortable acquaintance for him. He had numerous connections there besides Forney—George W. Childs, publisher of the *Public Ledger*; James Arnold, his bookbinder;

5. George Whitman's home, 431 Stevens Street, Camden

F. Gutekunst, his photographer; and many others. That spring he had written an essay for *Progress* about the sights of Chestnut Street.[4] And only the month before, he had gone over to West Philadelphia with Lou to escort Hattie and Jessie to the same train for their return to St. Louis after another of their visits in the East.[5]

Passing Twenty-second Street on the chessboard, he gave, we may surmise, more than a glancing thought to Anne Gilchrist, the English widow who in her admiration for *Leaves of Grass* had found a love for its author. Exactly three years earlier *to the day*, she had arrived in Philadelphia with her family. Later she had taken a house on North Twenty-second Street, and Whitman had frequently visited there, sometimes staying over for days at a time in a room reserved for him. Now Anne was back in England. Whitman had said his final goodbye to her three months before in New York City.[6]

However or wherever they formed their party, the four men—Forney, Reitzel, Martin, and Whitman—using passes Forney had obtained from the Pennsylvania Railroad,[7] boarded a "sleeper" at 9:10 that night.[8] At Lancaster Geist joined them;[9] then, not far past Harrisburg they turned in for the night, leaving the scenery of their mountainous route to the darkness.

The next morning, Thursday the eleventh, they were in Pittsburgh. Whitman thought the scene was in part "grim" (with respect to the houses he saw), but he deleted that observation when he rewrote his notes for *Specimen Days*: "Pretty good view of the city and Birmingham—fog and damp, smoke, coke-furnaces, flames, discolor'd wooden houses, and vast collections of coal-barges."[10]

Two years before, in July 1877, the Pittsburgh railroad yards had been a grim scene indeed. Striking trainmen, responding to wage cuts and other railroad economies, wound up facing National Guardsmen from Philadelphia. In the ensuing battle three or four soldiers and about nineteen civilians were killed, and much property lost. Numerous railroad cars and locomotives were destroyed by fire, as were many buildings, including two roundhouses, a nearby hotel, and Union Station.[11] If Whitman made any notes of remaining scars there, they are lost to us.

Following the route of the Pittsburgh, Cincinnati and St. Louis Railway, a branch of the Pennsylvania, the party crossed the Ohio River and the panhandle of West Virginia, then headed for Columbus.[12] It may have been on this stretch that the men began a series of discussions for which Forney and Whitman served in turn as "referees." One discussion (which must surely have included references to the 1877 strikes) was about the development of railroads in America. Martin cited the adage that "from the Delaware to the Allegheny the cities built the railroads, from the Allegheny to the Mississippi the railroads built the cities." He approved of the fact that railroads were "loosed westward" to "minister" to the unoccupied western lands.[13]

Forney, who had traveled in England and France for the Centennial Commission just a few years before, praised the Pullman Palace Car as a fine "specialty of this Western World," without peer in Europe. He recalled the "barbarisms of English railroad accommodations," and the "wretched cars" on the Continent.[14] What Geist and Reitzel contributed is not recorded. Whitman, however, their "referee,"

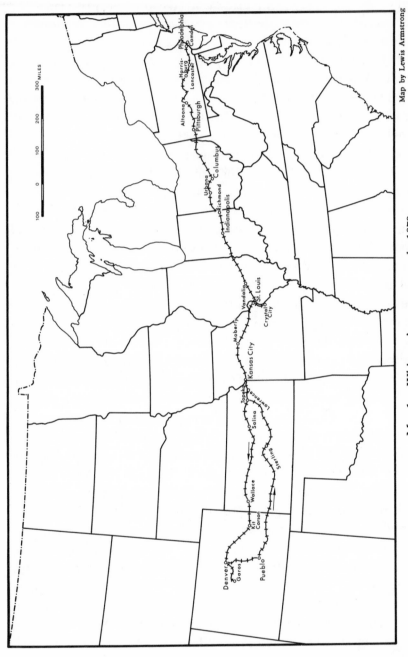

Map 1. Whitman's western travels, 1879

Map by Lewis Armstrong

wound up the discussion: "A railroad," he said, "means more than traffic and is wider in signifance than trade; it means the welding of the peoples, the harmonizing of thought, the interchange of mind as well as products; if it is not autocratic it is nothing, no autocrat in the world has been so potential for good."[15]

In *Specimen Days* Whitman reports that it was "a fierce weird pleasure to lie in my berth at night in the luxurious palace-car, drawn by the mighty Baldwin—embodying, and filling me, too, full of the swiftest motion, and most resistless strength!" He thought that if Voltaire had traveled by rail from New York to San Francisco he would have designated the American sleeper instead of the grand opera and a ship of war "the most signal illustration of the growth of humanity's and art's advance beyond primitive barbarism."[16]

In a time when railroad accidents were frequent, as the daily papers attest, the men were aware, of course, of a certain danger in their travel. A few years earlier Whitman had written to Peter Doyle, his streetcar conductor friend of the Washington days, that accidents "seem the fortune of RR travel, which I sometimes think more risky than the 'fortune of war.' "[17] In describing his 1879 travels in *Specimen Days*, though, he says he had decided that "the element of danger adds zest to it all."[18] That Thursday afternoon at about 5:30 he may have thought otherwise, however, for their train had a bad collision near Urbana, Ohio. As a local weekly reported the accident:

> Last Thursday evening train #5 on the Pan Handle road going east, found it necessary to go to the switch at the hoist, to give #10 the track, but omitted the precaution of sending a flagman ahead. Train #10 came around the curve, just as the other train had passed the hoist at the rate of forty miles an hour. The engineer of #5 backed his engine, and the engineer of #10 reversed his, but too late to avoid a collision that piled the engine of the west bound on top of the east bound train, mashing the engines and disturbing the passengers generally. A mail agent, E. W. Simpson, jumped from the train, and was about the only one hurt. A truck crushed [sic] into the hoist, carrying terror to those within. When the engines struck, train #5 was backing at the rate of about 15 miles per hour.[19]

Whitman wrote to Louisa that the accident "just escaped being something very bad indeed—the two locomotives all shivered to splinters—

nobody hurt however, (only one man who jumped, the mail agent) —detained us there 2½ hours—I didn't mind it at all."[20] It was later discovered that the mail car was damaged worse than was at first thought, so down the track at Richmond, Indiana, they lost further time while the mail was transferred to another car.[21]

That evening, after stopping for another change of engines at Indianapolis, the party continued on the "Vandalia Line" into the first of three impressive sunsets "over an hour each time" that Whitman recorded in his notebook: "One in Illinois west of Columbus; one at Tower Park St. Louis, and one crossing west Missouri. The golden sun & light blue clouds."[22] That second night he slept well, he wrote Louisa,[23] "flying like lightning through Illinois."[24]

Geist reported retiring that Thursday night in comfort and peace, then awaking at Vandalia, sixty-eight miles from St. Louis, "in time to see a fruitful and beautiful and one of the oldest settled sections of Illinois." Then, Highland, thirty-two miles from St. Louis, "as lovely as it is fertile in its surroundings, the undulating surface of the land affording a pleasant relief to the previously level stretch of prairie."[25]

At last the train reached the Mississippi River, crossed on the five-year-old East St. Louis bridge (the Eads Bridge), and ran through the tunnel to the Union Depot. Jeff was waiting and took them to the Planters' Hotel, where they had a "royal" breakfast of "perfect beefsteak, broiled chicken, oysters, good coffee, etc." which, Whitman wrote to Louisa, he enjoyed because he "hadn't eat any thing since yesterday at 3½."[26]

The Planters' Hotel, built in 1841, was at that time still one of the West's finer establishments. Geist reported that it was "one of the oldest but best kept hotels in the West, and elicited the praise of Charles Dickens in his 'American Notes,' when he stopped here."[27]

The party spent that Friday, the twelfth, and that night in St. Louis, all stopping at the Planters' except Whitman, who stayed over at Jeff's house.[28] That day Forney and Reitzel apparently went off on a separate excursion about the city with political and newspaper acquaintances. Ex-Senator David H. Armstrong and Joseph B. McCullagh, the editor of the *St. Louis Daily Globe-Democrat*, took them, among other places, to visit the home of the philanthropist Harry

6. Planters' Hotel, St. Louis, about 1879

Shaw, who had given his extensive botanical gardens to the city.[29] Jeff evidently drove the other three out to see Shaw's gardens also, and to see Tower Park, the fairgrounds, and the waterworks on a curve of the river northeast of town. Geist, who liked machinery, found Jeff's explanation of the operation of the waterworks so fascinating that he gave his Lancaster readers a full account of the system.[30] Martin reported in the *Press* the trade and traffic of St. Louis (then the fourth largest city in the country—after New York, Chicago, and Philadelphia), and noted the city's many fine buildings, including the St. Louis Club and the Chamber of Commerce buildings.[31] To Whitman it all must have seemed a vivid contrast with the St. Louis he and Jeff had briefly explored in 1848 on their return from New Orleans.

That afternoon both Forney and Whitman were interviewed by some of the newspapers; the reporters sought out Forney first. They were especially interested in his declared support of Grant for a third term in the presidency. One of the reporters made much of Forney's rapid-fire speaking style, his ability "to maintain a speed of over 200 words a minute in talking with an interviewer, and to stroke his English mutton-chop whiskers meantime."[32]

Whitman impressed them first by his appearance. The *Missouri Republican* reported: "Walt Whitman is a man well advanced in years and his snow-white hair and the long white beard which grows upon a large portion of his face give him a decidedly venerable appearance. He wore a gray traveling suit and his shirt bosom was left open at the neck, something after the fashion of the Goddess of Liberty as shown on a fifty-cent piece."[33]

Similarly, the *Globe-Democrat*'s man found Whitman "an oddity in his appearance as in his writings," and more "venerable" and "patriarchal" looking than the older Forney. His "quaint garb and primitive collar" also attracted the reporter's attention.[34]

From the interviews we get Whitman's view of himself as Forney's guest on the trip to Kansas, not as the Old Settlers' invited poet. He had agreed to go to the Lawrence meeting, he said, provided that he was not asked to speak nor eat any public dinners. He was "only to show himself" at the Silver Wedding in Kansas—"the people will have a chance to see this big, saucy red rooster, whom they otherwise think would speak."[35] He hoped to go on from there to Colorado, though that was not yet fully decided upon.[36] And after his trip he planned to lecture and read his own poems in public.[37]

The *Globe-Democrat* interview reveals other ways Whitman wanted the public to think of him at this time. For one thing, he wanted to be identified with the West: "I am called a Western man. Although born in New York, I am in sympathy and preference Western—better fitted for the Mississippi Valley."[38] And he hoped to be considered a comrade of the press: "I like to meet people, and especially the young men of the press. I think American boys are very companionable, the friendliest in the world. As I have noted in my poem, I think American youths, more than any other, are possessed of that high quality and gift, comradeship. But especially do I like to meet writers and young men of the craft. I am a printer, and can yet stick type with the average compositor."[39]

According to one of the reporters, Whitman's nieces "and other young ladies" picked him up for a carriage ride later that day. Perhaps it was on this ride that he saw the Tower Park sunset noted in his diary.[40]

The next morning, Saturday the thirteenth, at nine o'clock, the five men left via the St. Louis, Kansas City and Northern Railway for Kansas City. Now, instead of a sleeper, they had a car with reclining coach seats, which Geist thought very comfortable.[41] Whitman made detailed notes of this section of the trip:

> the RR we go on . . . is *the* (northern) *St Louis and Kansas City RR*, 275 miles (from St L to K C) right through the (northern) centre and natural beauty and richness of this great State. Cross'g the Missouri river on the bridge at the pretty town of St. Charles, we enter upon the finest soil, show (on a loose, slip-shod scale) trees, beauty, eligibility for tillage of crops, and general look of open air health, picturesqueness that I ever saw, and continue all day on the same enchant'g   nearly three hundred miles—ahead of any thing in Pennsylvania or New York states good as those are
>
> they raise a good deal of tobacco in these counties of Missouri, you see the light greenish-gray leaves pulled and now (Sept 13, '79) in great patches on rows of sticks or frameworks, hanging out to dry—looking like leaves of the mullein, familiar to eastern eyes.
>
> Yet, fine as it is, it isn't the finest part of the State. (There a bed of impervious clay and hard pan every where down below on this line, that holds the water—"drowns the land in wet weather, and bakes it in dry," as some one harshly said.) South are some rich counties; but the beauty spots are the north-western portions[42]

It is rewarding to see how Whitman later used these notes in *Specimen Days*. There he attempts to re-focus the experience on himself: "*I* sped on westward," "*I* cross'd Missouri State," "as a cynical farmer told *me*." He is less than skillful in re-handling the time: "now, and from what I have seen and learn'd since." And he awkwardly adds the details about the drying of tobacco after discussing the larger topic of Missouri "averaged politically and socially." Here is his account in *Specimen Days*:

> So merely stopping over night that time in St. Louis, I sped on

westward. As I cross'd Missouri State the whole distance by the St. Louis and Kansas City Northern Railroad, a fine early autumn day, I thought my eyes had never looked on scenes of greater pastoral beauty. For over two hundred miles successive rolling prairies, agriculturally perfect view'd by Pennsylvania and New Jersey eyes, and dotted here and there with fine timber. Yet fine as the land is, it isn't the finest portion; (there is a bed of impervious clay and hard-pan beneath this section that holds water too firmly, "drowns the land in wet weather, and bakes it in dry," as a cynical farmer told me.) South are some richer tracts, though perhaps the beauty-spots of the State are the northwestern counties. Altogether, I am clear (now, and from what I have seen and learn'd since,) that Missouri, in climate, soil, relative situation, wheat, grass, mines, railroads, and every important materialistic respect, stands in the front rank of the Union. Of Missouri averaged politically and socially I have heard all sorts of talk, some pretty severe—but I should have no fear myself of getting along safely and comfortably anywhere among the Missourians. They raise a good deal of tobacco. You see at this time quantities of the light greenish-gray leaves pulled and hanging out to dry on temporary frameworks or rows of sticks. Looks much like the mullein familiar to eastern eyes.[43]

It was probably on this stretch that the party encountered the peddler in the cars "selling candies, papers, books, etc." As Whitman recalled the episode years later, amused at what he called being "set back," the peddler "made dead set at me and the party I was with to buy a book. 'Go away, my son,' I said. 'Go away, go away. *We* don't want books, we write books ourselves.' 'Books!' he said. 'What sort of books? Almanacs?' "[44]

At Lexington Junction, forty miles from Kansas City, at about eight o'clock that evening, they stopped for dinner. Geist thought the meal the best they had had at a railroad station, "with attention from landlord and servants to match." He was reminded of home meals when company was present: "The prairie fowls and sirloin were done to a fault; the waffles were superb; while the coffee was so unlike what travelers are usually compelled to imagine to be coffee that the contrast was really refreshing. And then there were so many side dishes to discuss, notably some home-made chow-chow. . . ." The men enjoyed their meal so much that the conductor allowed them an added twenty minutes "to allow our Orator and Poet to digest an extra waffle."[45]

They didn't realize as they took their good time in Lexington Junction that a committee of the Old Settlers would be in Kansas City waiting to meet them. They had planned when they got there to stay at the Coates House "with our old-time Lancaster county friend, Colonel Kersey Coates," Geist had written earlier.[46] But when they arrived at the station they were met by George A. Crawford and five other Kansans, along with Stephen Smart of the Kansas Pacific Railway—and with a KP train waiting to take them to Lawrence.[47] Martin reported that when Whitman met these western escorts, he remarked quietly, "Well, gentlemen, I see you do not wear pistols."[48]

3

TO THE THREE HUNDRED AND FIFTY THOUSAND
OWNERS OF SLAVES

Suppose you get Kansas, do you think it would be ended?
Suppose you and the politicians put Buchanan into the Eighteenth
Presidency, or Fillmore into the Presidency, do you think it would
be ended? I know nothing more desirable for those who contend
against you than that you should get Kansas. Then would the melt
begin in These States that would not cool till Kansas should be
redeemed, as of course it would be.

"The Eighteenth Presidency!" 1856

Whitman & the Kansas Silver Wedding

At Lawrence, Kansas, which the Forney party reached around one o'clock in the morning, one of the sons of Mayor John P. Usher, probably John, Jr., met the train and, as Geist said, "claimed our orator and poet as his special guests."[1] The other three went to the Ludington House, "the best hotel in the city," which Geist compared favorably with the Stevens House in Lancaster.[2]

When Forney and Whitman arrived at Usher's house, a two-story Italianate structure on Tennessee Street, they signed the guest register. Whitman wrote:

> Walt Whitman
> visiting Kansas
> Sept. 14, 1879[3]

Whether the senior Ushers were still awake to greet them at that early morning hour is not recorded.

John P. Usher was at this time the general solicitor for the Kansas Pacific Railway. He had been Lincoln's secretary of the interior, following Caleb Smith in that position. It is likely that the last time Whitman had seen him was in mid-May of 1865 when Usher left the secretaryship a month after Lincoln's assassination. At that time, at a farewell session at the Patent Office, he was presented with a scroll of appreciation signed by his employees, including Whitman, who since January of that year had been serving in the Indian Bureau.[4] Now the former clerk was a guest in Usher's home.

7. Home of John P. Usher, Lawrence

That Sunday, the fourteenth, Whitman apparently did not go, as did Geist and Martin, to hear Edward Everett Hale preach at the Congregational Church.[5] Instead, for a good part of the day he rested and enjoyed the hospitality of the Ushers in their well-appointed home.[6] Probably sometime that day, perhaps after dinner, Usher and his guests reminisced over the Civil War years in Washington. And perhaps the talk got around to Usher's successor as secretary of the interior, James Harlan of Iowa, who had dismissed Whitman from the department six weeks after Usher's departure. Harlan, having seen a copy of *Leaves of Grass* Whitman kept in his desk (the 1860 "Blue Book"), had judged the work indecent, and so fired its author.[7]

Evidently there was some sightseeing that day also. Linton Usher, the third son, who was twenty-seven at the time, years later remembered going on at least one carriage ride with Whitman.[8] Perhaps it

28

was that afternoon he visited the campus of the four-hundred student University of Kansas and, as Whitman says he did, looked over the surrounding countryside from Mt. Oread.[9]

That afternoon he may also have seen Lawrence all decked out for the Silver Wedding celebration. A large banner across Massachusetts Street read, "1854—Old Settlers Welcome—1879." Private homes and business places were decorated with Chinese lanterns, green boughs, and red, white, and blue bunting. Flags were everywhere: the *Daily Journal* stretched a forty-footer across the street in front of its shop. Someone put out a Union flag, another a German one. A butcher stuck small flags over some quarters of beef hanging on display. A dry goods store showed long rolls of red, white, and blue flannel; a clothing store had a similarly patriotic display of men's shirts. Here and there placards reminded visitors of Lawrence's past: "Site of Old Free State Hotel" (on the Ludington House), "All Quantrell [sic] Left in this Block" (on a harness shop).[10]

Lawrence, a city of between eight and nine thousand, was bulging with visitors. Private homes were filled with guests, and the hotels were jammed. The Ludington House, where Geist, Martin, and Reitzel were staying, even rented its billiard tables for berths.[11] And on Monday the streets were "thronged with pedestrians, horsemen, parties in hacks, carriages, buggies, busses, all turned in the direction of Bismarck Grove."[12]

The wooden toll bridge across the Kansas River, declared free for the two days of the celebration, almost didn't serve at all. A week before, the north span had collapsed under the pitching and crowding of about one hundred and fifty cattle, part of a drive headed for northern Missouri. For a time it had appeared that the Old Settlers would have to make do with a ferry, but by heroic efforts they got a temporary span in place by the weekend.[13]

Bismarck Grove was just across the river about a mile and a half to the northeast, in the former Delaware Indian lands, owned in 1879 by the Kansas Pacific. For a number of seasons it had been little more than a picnic grove for the families of the railroad's employees who worked in nearby shops. In the few years before the Quarter Centennial, however, it had been developed by the railroad into a convention

8. Massachusetts Street, Lawrence, 1870s

center with walks and drives among its elms and walnut trees, and with, among other facilities, its own railroad depot and a thousand-seat "tabernacle." Earlier that year the Temperance Society had met there, as had a Sunday-school chautauqua and the National Liberal League, an organization dedicated to the separation of church and state.[14]

At sunrise Monday morning a brass twelve-pound cannon was fired in salute twenty-five times. Geist, so suddenly awakened, half dreamed that there had been an explosion at the *New Era* printshop.[15] Then, with all of Lawrence's bells ringing, the two-day celebration got under way.

The weather Monday was "beautiful"—"a perfect Kansas day" with a breeze from the northwest and a 2 P.M. temperature of only seventy-four degrees. The next day was not that comfortable; the wind came out of the southwest, driving up the thermometer to eighty-three

9. Bismarck Grove (two halves of a single panoramic view), 1880

31

degrees.[16] Attendance at the grove both days was estimated by the Lawrence papers to be around thirty thousand. On Tuesday, someone estimated, over a thousand vehicles had crossed over the bridge that morning, creating a serious parking problem at the grove. The crowd was "simply awful," one reporter wrote. The tabernacle was packed.[17] Despite the crowding, the throng was by all accounts an orderly one. Forney and Geist both wrote of their surprise at the "unconstrained temperance" of the men at the meeting, and of the absence of liquor, beer, and wine.[18] Forney also reported on the number of attractive men and women at the grove (in Topeka he was to see "well-developed, graceful ladies"), and wrote that Kansans talked "with the clear precision of New England and the sturdy sense of Pennsylvania."[19]

The two-day program divided much speech-making with music, singing, and poetry. The surviving members of the old 1850s "first band" of Lawrence played together again.[20] The tabernacle throng sang, and sang again, a hymn to "Old John Brown."[21] A trio from Larned sang Henry Clay Work's "Song of a Thousand Years."[22] Some poems were also sung, including verses by Lucy Larcom and by her mentor, John Greenleaf Whittier. The celebrants sang lines of Whittier's "Randolph of Roanoke" ("O MOTHER EARTH! upon thy lap/ Thy weary ones receiving"), and of his "Kansas Emigrants":

> We cross the prairie as of old
> The pilgrims crossed the sea,
> To make the West, as they the East,
> The homestead of the free![23]

Whittier had been invited to the Silver Wedding as one whose Kansas credentials were widely recognized. In both prose and poetry, out of a long-held interest in the "prairied West," Whittier had fought against the extension of slavery into the state. He would have been a fine symbolic figure on the speakers' platform, but the seventy-two-year-old poet had to write back to the Old Settlers that he had "not health and strength for the journey."[24]

Another feature of the Silver Wedding was the Grand Barbecue provided free on Tuesday. An ox was roasted (with "hogs, sheep, and other good things") under a large tin reflector specially constructed for the occasion. It looked, someone thought, like an inverted bathtub. The feast was a huge one, with thousands lining up before three carvers, then dining at long tables or on the grass under the trees.[25]

The oratory, however, was the main show. Ex-Governor Charles Robinson made the first welcoming address. Robinson, who had been Kansas's first state governor, gave what amounted to a keynote speech, for he recalled the struggle to keep Kansas free from slavery. His Free Soil theme was picked up by other welcoming speakers: by Mayor Usher, by Governor John P. St. John, and by Cyrus K. Holliday, who, with Robinson, had been one of the founders of Topeka. The same note ran through the several impromptu speeches given on Monday night at what was billed as a Love Feast. At that session the old-timers were "called out" to tell of their experiences in the territorial days.[26]

Free Soil was also the theme of the two principal guest speakers, Forney and Hale. Forney, introduced by Crawford, recalled the great struggle to keep Kansas free. He recited his and other Pennsylvanians' contributions to that cause. And he called on the South to seek more liberal means to become prosperous in freedom as Kansas had done.[27] Edward Everett Hale, a Unitarian minister, also had had a personal stake in the free-state struggle, for he had worked for the New England Emigrant Aid Company, a main force in the settling of Kansas by antislavery men. Hale's speech, on New England's contributions toward Kansas's free-state status, provided an appropriate counterpoint to Forney's on the Pennsylvania role.[28]

The Old Settlers didn't have Whittier, but Forney had brought them Whitman. On Monday he sat on the platform near Forney and Hale. The latter had been one of the few friendly critics of the 1855 *Leaves of Grass;* we must wonder if Whitman remembered that.[29] A reporter thought the poet one of the most noticeable men there, "venerable in appearance, with white flowing beard and open shirtcollar."[30] Forney wrote that "with his white coronal" Whitman "sat there like an ancient Druid . . . and, though he wrote no hymns, spoke in no uncertain joy at the sight of the athletic throngs."[31]

Whitman also had good Kansas credentials, though probably few of the Old Settlers realized it. As a newspaperman in his early days he had been a Free-Soil spokesman, most notably as editor of the

Brooklyn Freeman.[32] His *Leaves of Grass* had celebrated western settlement. Two of his poems, "The Mystic Trumpeter" and "Virginia—The West," had appeared first in the *Kansas Magazine* of 1872.[33] In his *Democratic Vistas* (1870) he had envisioned "the dominion heart of America . . . far inland, toward the West."[34] And, as has been noted, he described himself in St. Louis as "in sympathy and preference Western."[35]

Somehow, despite Whitman's plan to do little more than present himself at the Silver Wedding, and despite the fact that he was there by Forney's invitation and as his traveling companion only, he found himself expected to deliver a poem on Tuesday.[36] He failed to show up then, however, and the man who was to introduce him, T. Dwight Thacher, editor of the *Lawrence Daily Journal*, explained that

> the state of Mr. Whitman's health precludes the possibility of his presence here to-day, and deprives us of the privilege of listening to the poem which we had hoped to hear from his own lips. He was present yesterday, but the fatigues of travel and the excitement of the occasion have precluded his presence here to-day. Had he been here, I should perhaps have said in introducing him that I first met him in New York many years ago, when the Kansas struggle for liberty was still being waged, and his sympathies were all on our side. How could they have been otherwise? Despotism does not produce poets. It takes the love of liberty to produce either poems or poets.[37]

The day before, one of the *Journal's* reporters had noted that the poet appeared in "feeble health" and perhaps would not be able "to read a poem as expected to."[38] It may have been that a very tired Whitman, having no real obligation to the Old Settlers, decided on an uncomfortably hot day to stay at Usher's house and avoid not only another platform appearance but also the Grand Barbecue.

In his old age Linton Usher recalled that the poet was not well, and that he and John, Jr., entertained him with accounts of western life.[39] Linton had from an early age roamed widely in the West—his "Wilderness University," he called it.[40] His description of ranch life in Texas, he remembered, greatly interested Whitman.[41] In *Specimen Days* the poet says he had had "such a good time and rest, and talk and dinner" with Usher's sons that he had "let the hours slip away and didn't drive over to the meeting."[42]

He had been "erroneously billed to deliver a poem," Whitman says in *Specimen Days*. He still hadn't a poem ready, but since something was expected of him, and he "wanted to be good-natured," he had "hastily pencill'd" a short speech. He had planned to tell the Old Settlers, among other things, how much he was impressed by the land—

> that feature of the topography of your western central world—that vast Something, stretching out on its own unbounded scale, unconfined, which there is in these prairies, combining the real and ideal, and beautiful as dreams.
>
> I wonder indeed if the people of this continental inland West know how much of first-class *art* they have in these prairies—how original and all your own—how much of the influences of a character for your future humanity, broad, patriotic, heroic and new? how entirely they tally on land the grandeur and superb monotony of the skies of heaven, and the ocean with its waters? how freeing, soothing, nourishing they are to the soul?
>
> Then is it not subtly they who have given us our leading modern Americans, Lincoln and Grant?—vast-spread, average men—their foregrounds of character altogether practical and real, yet (to those who have eyes to see) with finest backgrounds of the ideal, towering high as any. And do we not see, in them, foreshadowings of the future races that shall fill these prairies?[43]

The Silver Wedding ended that night, with the bells of Lawrence pealing anew, this time signaling many farewells. Whitman signed the Usher guest book again, this time to note his departure:

> Walt Whitman
> accompanying Col. Forney as above
> Sept. 16, '79[44]

4

VIRGINIA—THE WEST

The noble sire fallen on evil days,
I saw with hand uplifted, menacing, brandishing,
(Memories of old in abeyance, love and faith in abeyance,)
The insane knife toward the Mother of All.

The noble son on sinewy feet advancing,
I saw, out of the land of prairies, land of Ohio's waters, and of
    Indiana,
To the rescue the stalwart giant hurry his plenteous offspring,
Drest in blue, bearing their trusty rifles on their shoulders.

Then the Mother of All with calm voice speaking,
As to you Rebellious, (I seemed to hear her say,) why strive against
    me, and why seek my life?
When you yourself forever provide to defend me?
For you provided me Washington—and now these also.

Leaves of Grass, 1881

Topeka & Westward to Denver

Rail traffic between Lawrence and Topeka was so heavy at the conclusion of the Silver Wedding that the Kansas Pacific had to fit out a baggage car with chairs for the Forney party that Tuesday night. The men were in good company, however, for they rode with state officers, including judges of the supreme court, and with General Galusha Pennypacker, a friend of Forney's and the commanding general at Fort Riley to the west. The train was late in departing, so they didn't arrive in Topeka until about 8:30.[1]

At Topeka the train was met by the Capital Guards Band. According to one newspaper: "Col. Forney and Hon. Walt Whitman, our distinguished visitors who came upon the train," were escorted to the Tefft House. "Amid the roar of fireworks, booming of cannon, clamor of horns and tread of horses and men, the scene partook somewhat, for a while, of agony and style, enough to impress the honorable gentlemen from abroad that they were not in a desert or wilderness uninhabited."[2]

With a population of over fifteen thousand, Topeka was almost twice as large as Lawrence.[3] Whitman later described both places as "large, bustling, half-rural, handsome cities."[4] Forney found Topeka a "busy, clean, cheerful city," with wide avenues, churches "like small cathedrals," and "stores that would do credit to Chestnut Street." Prices were low, too; he reported that Martin "bought a hat for four dollars that would have cost six dollars in Philadelphia."[5]

On Wednesday, Whitman and his friends toured the new capitol, only the east wing of which had been completed. They visited several

10. Tefft House, Topeka

offices: the state printer, the department of education, the office of Chief Justice Horton, the historical society, and the board of agriculture.[6] At the last place, the journalists were presented with copies of the agricultural yearbook, filled with crop production figures that fully supported the good impression Kansas had made as an agricultural state at the Philadelphia exposition three years before.[7]

They also had interviews with Governor John P. St. John. The governor was pleased to spend time with representatives of the eastern press, for he wanted publicity for his Freedmen's Relief Association then seeking funds to assist the Exodusters. These were blacks fleeing the repressive South to what they thought would be a New Canaan in Kansas. St. John showed them numerous letters from the South attesting to the need for help, and all three—Forney, Geist, and Martin—gave his cause full coverage in their papers.[8] It is perhaps in the context of "the Negro Exodus" (as Geist's paper headlined his interview with St. John) that we can interpret a scrawled note Whitman made at this time: "not many blacks," it appears to read.[9]

Other sights that day were Washburn College, the College of the Sisters of Bethany, and the newly built City Hall, where Mayor M. H. Case described his modernization of the fire department.[10] Geist was reported as calling at the offices of the *Commonwealth*.[11] He also made a special excursion to visit the poorer sections of the city where he found, he said, the people "in good health and spirits, with plenty to do, and full of hope for the future."[12]

It isn't definite how much of all this touring, beyond the visit to the capitol, Whitman participated in—his daybook mentions a ride about the city; *Specimen Days* reports "two or three long drives" about Topeka, and "the brotherly kindness of my RR. friends there, and the city and State officials."[13] In his notebook jottings he cites, more specifically, "many kindnesses" indebting him to Mayor Case, Governor St. John, and Stephen F. Smart.[14] One of the Topeka papers reported his visit to the capitol on Wednesday, and in another item for that day said that he "sat most of the time in the office of the Tefft House . . . , and met several gentlemen with whom he conversed pleasantly."[15]

That same day Mayor Case issued this public notice:

> The Capital Guards of this city are hereby permitted to have the use of Kansas Avenue between Fifth and Eighth Streets, from the hours of 7 to 8 o'clock this Wednesday evening, September 17th, for the purpose of a military display, including a sham battle, in honor of the distinguished friends of Kansas, Col. John W. Forney, Walt. Whitman and party, who have favored the State and the Capital with their first visit.
>
> The City Marshal, all policemen and citizens will govern themselves accordingly.
>
> M. H. Case, Mayor[16]

11. Kansas Statehouse, Topeka, 1879

Mayor Case had second thoughts about the display, fearing danger "to life and property," for he later revoked the order. He was persuaded to reinstate it, however, and the affair went ahead. The guards, headed by the band, marched up Kansas Avenue to the Tefft House at Seventh Street. There, with Whitman and his friends seated on the balcony, they did "several neat movements," including the manual of arms. Then they put on a sham battle, "and for a few moments a well directed fusilade (blank cartridges) was sent into the imaginary enemy. The firing was done with great regularity and evidenced the perfection in drill which the Guards have attained." There was also a bayonet charge, and while the battle was going forward the band played at the corner. There were no accidents, the papers reported. "All horses were removed from the streets and small boys kept out of harm's way." At

12. Kansas Avenue, Topeka, 1876; Tefft House at left

8:30, by invitation the guards and the band went to the Opera House to hear Forney give a lecture.[17]

Forney's address at the Opera House, on "Some of the Public Men of America I Have Known," had been well advertised in the Topeka papers, and the public had to a certain extent been given the expectation that Whitman would be a guest on the stage. George A. Crawford had told the *Commonwealth* that Forney was a fine figure, and that "to see him and Walt Whitman on the stand together, will be worth the price of admission to the Opera House Wednesday, if nothing whatever is said."[18] On the sixteenth the *Daily Blade* had stated that "Hon. Walt. Whitman, the poet, will be in Topeka tomorrow and will be on the stage at Forney's lecture tomorrow night."[19] For all the advertising, and even with the guards as guests, Forney's lecture drew an audience to fill only about two-thirds of the house seats. Whitman was not reported as being on the stage, though the newspapers in their rather full coverage listed the several who were, including Governor St. John (who introduced Forney), Justice Horton, Bishop Vail, and George A. Crawford.[20]

Thursday the men were invited to a midday farewell banquet at the Palace Hotel near the Kansas Pacific depot across the Kansas River.

They took an omnibus from the Tefft House, and while crossing the bridge saw "a number of Indians watering their ponies in the river." This may have been the party of about twenty Potawatomi elsewhere reported as passing through that day "on their way to the Nation for a deer hunt."[21] According to the *Commonwealth* the sight of the Indians was a curiosity to the easterners, and one which had to be investigated: "Accordingly, when the 'bus was about halfway across the bridge they alighted, and returning, scrambled down the bank and said 'how' to the red men. It is possible that these hungry-looking specimens of Indian braves dispelled much of the sentiment eastern people indulge in, when speaking of Mr. Lo."[22] It may have been this incident that prompted Whitman to jot down these notes: "Chief Wapalingna / died 2 years ago / 116 years of age / a brave blind Indian / never spoke English / The squad of Indians / at Topeka / Mr Smart on / the Indians."[23]

There is another story of Whitman meeting Indians in Topeka, a story he told the sculptor Sidney H. Morse years later. According to Morse, the sheriff invited the Forney party down to the jail to see about twenty Indian prisoners in the jailyard:

> The sheriff went out and spoke to them; told them of the distinguished party there, but they paid no attention. Forney went out and others followed . . . . But no look or word from the dusky prisoners except the first side-glance. Then Walt Whitman went out. The old chief looked at him steadily, then extended his hand and said his "how." All the other Indians followed, surrounded Whitman, shaking hands, making the air melodious with their "hows." The sheriff could not understand it. "I confess," said Walt Whitman, relating this story, "that I was not a little set up to find that the critters knew the difference and didn't confound me with the big guns of officialism."[24]

The farewell banquet was given by the Kansas Pacific in the persons of Stephen F. Smart and E. C. Devereux, Ticket Agent. One newspaper reported it as "A Feast of Reason and a Flow of Soul" for "Walt Whitman and party." Besides Whitman's group, the paper said, the invited guests were: Dr. W. K. Douglas, a minister from Mississippi; Governor St. John; Mayor Case; George A. Crawford; George

13. Kansas Pacific Railway advertising poster

W. Reed, editor of the *Topeka Blade*; and Major J. K. Hudson, editor of the *Topeka Capital*. The editor of the *Commonwealth* had also been invited, but was unable to attend. After the dinner, "a sumptuous repast," the guests had about an hour's conversation before their trains.[25]

Around 2:30 that afternoon, the eighteenth, Forney said goodbye to the others, and headed east with Devereux.[26] The four—Geist, Martin, Reitzel, and Whitman—had accepted invitations (and presumably passes) to travel on to Colorado, going out by way of the Kansas Pacific and returning on the Atchison, Topeka and Santa Fe Railroad.[27] Shortly after Forney's departure they headed west on the "Fast Denver Express." They were accompanied by Smart, who stayed with them about 450 miles of the way, until their train met an eastbound one the next day—probably between Kit Carson and Hugo, Colorado. Their route westward took them, as Geist reported it, first along the Kansas River (the "Kaw"), through Silver Lake, Kingsville, Rossville, St. Marys (where they saw the "magnificent brick structure" of the Seminary of the Sacred Heart), Wamego, St. George, and Manhattan ("the seat of the Agriculture College and Experimental Farm, an institution which is on the high road to practical success"). After Ogden

14. Hotel and depot, Wallace, 1875

46

they passed Fort Riley, and Geist gave a symbolic wave to General Pennypacker, whom they had left back in Topeka at the Tefft House.[28]

At Abilene they stopped for supper. Geist thought the dining facilities better than on any line he knew in the East. "And, what is specially notable, is that the hungry traveller is given ample time to get a good square meal. Even the landlords seem to sympathise with your keen appetite, as they take the trouble to remind you that you have plenty of time to take another cup of coffee or an extra biscuit or antelope steak."[29]

From Abilene they started across the "Golden Belt" of wheat-producing counties. After a stop at Salina they traveled at night, passing Bavaria, Brookville, Terra Cotta, Fort Harker, Ellsworth (the locale of a frontier shooting incident Whitman hears about). They went past Russell, Victoria, Hays City, Ellis, and WaKeeney (where, presumably, James F. Keeney, a fellow-passenger and one of the town's founders, disembarked). In the morning they arrived at Wallace at a depot hotel for breakfast. Geist found the place a "delightful and healthful summer resort"—a stop-over for invalids on their way to Colorado.[30] That state was just beginning to be developed as a place for cures. As Whitman wrote to Louisa, he noticed on his train a "very sick lady" whose husband was taking her to Colorado, "hoping it will help her."[31]

At Wallace, Whitman may have observed soldiers from Fort Wallace, about a mile and a half to the southeast. Perhaps by way of some military remembrance he was prompted to give Smart these lines for the Old Settlers' record of their meeting:

> Not a grave of the murdered for Freedom
> But grows seeds of a wider Freedom,
> Which the winds carry afar and sow,
> And the snows and the rains nourish.

He had first published these lines in a New York newspaper in 1850, five years before he incorporated them in somewhat altered form in the first edition of *Leaves of Grass*. They became the epigraph for the *Kansas Memorial*, the official report of the Silver Wedding.[32]

Whitman made several notes about the next stretch of the journey, notes which he later edited for *Specimen Days*. His jottings at the time:

Friday Sept 19 '79 / on *the Plains* (western / edge of Kansas, on to Col / orado) — plains — plains — plains / The dugouts / antelope / the Prairie-dog / emigrant wagons / camped for the night / the vast stretching plains / hundreds of miles area / the buffalo grass / the yellow wild flowers / the rare [struck over], clear, pure / cool, rarified air /(over 3000 ft above / sea level) the dry rivers / the ant hill / the buffalo wallow / the cow boys ("cow / punchers") [indecipherable strikeover] to me / a wonderfully interesting / class — clear swarthy complexion — with / broad brimm'd hats — their / loose arms always slightly / raised & swinging as they ride — their / splendid eyes — (Fra Diavolo / & his men in the opera) / — a herd of horses / numbering 200 / Tongahocksa / Monotony / Eagle Tail after a / chief / Mirage / see mirages, train of / cars / Agate / signs of fires / a cedar woods ridge / the long furrow / for fire-guard / an occasional corral[33]

The long Wallace-to-Denver part of the trip was broken by a stop for another "excellent dinner" (in Geist's estimation), this one at Hugo, Colorado.[34] They arrived in Denver that Friday evening, the nineteenth, at 4:30,[35] in time to see the mountains at sunset.[36]

5

SPIRIT THAT FORM'D THIS SCENE
Written in Platte Cañon, Colorado

Spirit that form'd this scene,
These tumbled rock-piles grim and red,
These reckless heaven-ambitious peaks,
These gorges, turbulent-clear streams, this naked freshness,
These formless wild arrays, for reasons of their own,
I know thee, savage spirit—we have communed together,
Mine too such wild arrays, for reasons of their own;
Was't charged against my chants they had forgotten art?
To fuse within themselves its rules precise and delicatesse?
The lyrist's measur'd beat, the wrought-out temple's grace—
    column and polish'd arch forgot?
But thou that revelest here—spirit that form'd this scene,
They have remember'd thee.

Leaves of Grass, 1881

49

Denver & the Rockies

Denver in 1879 was prospering. Silver strikes at Leadville and elsewhere were creating new wealth in the area, the smelters were busy, the railroads, growing in number, were bringing in a great trade, along with thousands of people seeking health cures. The city was burgeoning; the census the next year would show a population of 35,600. In 1879 Denver had a streetcar system and two telephone companies, and was about to install electric lights.[1]

The three-story American House, at the corner of Blake and Sixth Streets, where Whitman's party stayed, was perhaps the city's finest hotel. Built in 1868, just as railroads were about to arrive in Denver, it was thought at that time almost too fine for the frontier city. Its broad stairway had a rich wine red carpet. Room furnishings were of walnut and plush and silk. The beds had feather mattresses, and rooms were provided with portable metal bathtubs (filled from pitchers). There was a spacious dining room, a glittering all-night bar, and a ballroom that became Denver's social center—its most auspicious event occurring seven years before Whitman's arrival, when a lavish ball was given there for the Grand Duke Alexis of Prussia.[2]

Leadville, a day's farther travel to the southwest, had become by that fall a magnet attracting a hundred or more arrivals daily.[3] Helping to speed them there were railroad advertisements such as those Whitman had undoubtedly seen in the Kansas papers, describing Leadville as a "rich opening" of "vast deposits" of silver near the surface, requiring for the taking only "muscle, energy and daily bread."[4] In

15. American House, Denver

1879, the "fever" year, Leadville was growing from a population of about eight thousand to one approaching thirty thousand.[5] It was the archetypal western boomtown. We can imagine its attraction to Whitman and his eastern journalist friends.

At first glance the records do suggest that Whitman made the excursion from Denver to Leadville. Marked maps indicating his travels he later sent to John Burroughs and to Anne Gilchrist do not pinpoint Leadville, but Whitman's tracings on them indicate that he ventured into the Rockies far south of Denver.[6] In what were evidently press releases the poet sent back to at least two eastern newspapers, the *Washington Evening Star* and the *Philadelphia Times*, he reported himself as fraternizing "with emigrant camps, miners, cow-boys, and Leadvilleans."[7] In *Specimen Days* he writes: "One of my pleasantest days was a jaunt, via Platte cañon, to Leadville." He begins the immediately following entry: "Jottings from the Rocky Mountains, mostly pencill'd during a day's trip over the South Park RR., returning from Leadville . . . ."[8]

Much as Whitman may have wished to visit Leadville, or to leave the impression he had visited that phenomenal place, his westward travels ended a mountain range short of it. To get to Leadville most directly that latter part of September, one took the narrow-gauge Denver, South Park and Pacific Railroad, the "South Park," still under construction. The route was by way of Platte Canyon to Webster, thence over ten-thousand-foot Kenosha Pass into South Park. At Red Hill one took a stage via Fairplay and Mosquito Pass to Leadville. Another way was to go to the end of the track at Guiraud, present-day Garos, and take the stage over Weston Pass.[9] Leadville would not have rail service until the following summer.[10] That September passengers from Denver still had to endure a harrowing thirty-five-mile stage ride through South Park and up over Mosquito Range. It was a jolting ride of four hours or more over a rough and hazardous road etched on the sides of the mountains, a ride through dust or mud, along terrifying precipices, and sometimes made in the fear of hold-ups.[11]

Whitman at sixty was no longer the man to make that last rugged part of the journey by stage. His note to Louisa on arrival in Denver that he was "feeling well—better than before I started" may be taken as indicative of his continuing concern (and hers) about his health.[12] Whatever his reason for missing the second day of the Silver Wedding in Kansas, it is not surprising that the "half-Paralytic" gave up an opportunity, as Martin put it, "to plunge 140 miles into the Rocky Mountains," and settled instead for visiting "points more accessible."[13] Geist reported their plans specifically:

> At Denver, Mr. Martin and myself accepted the invitation of Capt. Wm. T. Tough to visit that latest marvel of mining towns, Leadville, 140 miles distant, lying in a basin adjoining the backbone or divide of the Rocky Mountains, and distant only about 800 miles from San Francisco. As our route involved thirty-five miles of staging through the South Park and over "Mosquito Pass," the highest wagon road in the world, and a very tiresome ride, Mr. Whitman

concluded to remain in Denver until our return, and Mr. Reitzel having some business matters to transact, it was arranged that they should meet us on our return on Monday, at "The End of the Track" (Guyraud) of the Denver, South Park and Pacific railroad, 115 miles from Denver . . . .[14]

So, that Saturday, while Geist and Martin went to Leadville, Reitzel attended to some business, and Whitman took in the city. In *Specimen Days* he gives his impressions. He liked best what he saw of the men, "three-fourths of them, large, able, calm, alert, American." He was impressed by a visit to a smelting works where he saw silver turned into two-thousand-dollar bricks, and he liked the sights of the city itself:

> A city, this Denver, well-laid out—Laramie [sic] street, and 15th and 16th and Champa streets, with others, particularly fine—some with tall storehouses of stone or iron, and windows of plate-glass— all the streets with little canals of mountain water running along the sides—plenty of people, "business," modernness—yet not without a certain racy wild smack, all its own. A place of fast horses, (many mares with their colts,) and I saw lots of big greyhounds for antelope hunting. Now and then groups of miners, some just come in, some starting out, very picturesque.[15]

Sometime that Saturday, the twentieth, Whitman also wrote a press release that evidently appeared in the *Denver Daily Tribune* the next day. In *Specimen Days* a part of it is presented as an "off-hand" interview in which he is reported as saying:

> I have lived in or visited all the great cities in the Atlantic third of the republic—Boston, Brooklyn with its hills, New Orleans, Baltimore, stately Washington, broad Philadelphia, teeming Cincinnati and Chicago, and for thirty years in that wonder, wash'd by hurried and glittering tides, my own New York, not only the New World's but the world's city—but, newcomer to Denver as I am, and threading its streets, breathing its air, warm'd by its sunshine, and having what there is of its human as well as aerial ozone flash'd upon me now for only three or four days, I am very much like a man feels sometimes toward certain people he meets with, and warms to, and hardly knows why. I, too, can hardly tell why, but as I enter'd the city in the slight haze of a late September afternoon, and have breath'd its air, and slept well o' nights, and have roam'd or rode

16. Larimer Street, Denver, 1870s

leisurely, and watch'd the comers and goers at the hotels, and absorb'd the climatic magnetism of this curiously attractive region, there has steadily grown upon me a feeling of affection for the spot, which, sudden as it is, has become so definite and strong that I must put it on record.[16]

What is remarkable about this "interview" is not only that he wrote it himself, but that parts of it, omitted from *Specimen Days*, are identical with his undelivered "hastily scribbl'd" speech for the Old Settlers, as is evident in this item in the *Camden Daily Post*:

> Walt Whitman has been interviewed by the Denver *Tribune*, and among other things laudatory of Denver, Colorado, and the West generally, spoke of the Prairies (under which he grouped all the Central States) as a new and original influence in coloring humanity, and in art and literature. "These limitless and beautiful landscapes," he said, "indeed fill me best and most, and will longest remain with me, of all the objective shows I see on this my first visit to the Central States—the grand interior. I wonder if the people of the prairies know how much *art*, original and all their own, they have in those rolling and grassy plains—what a profound cast and bearing they will have on their coming populations and races, broader, newer, more patriotic, more heroic than ever before—giving a racy flavor and stamp to the United States of the future, and encouraging and compacting all. No wonder the Prairies have given the Nation its two leading modern typical men, Lincoln and Grant, of a vast average of elements of characters a[l]together practical and real, yet to subtler observation, with shaded backgrounds of the ideal, lofty and fervid as any."[17]

On Monday, Whitman and Reitzel arose early and took the eight o'clock "South Park" train up Platte Canyon, stopping for a "good breakfast of eggs, trout, and rice griddle cakes" at its entrance. The mountain canyon, like the wide plains of the days before, "tallied" with the poet's soul. "I have found the law of my own poems," he felt as the train made its way up the gorge "amid all this grim yet joyous elemental abandon—this plenitude of material, entire absence of art, untrammel'd play of primitive Nature—the chasm, the gorge, the crystal mountain stream . . . the fantastic forms, bathed in transparent browns, faint reds and grays, towering sometimes a thousand, sometimes two or three thousand feet high—at their tops now and then huge masses pois'd, and mixing with the clouds, with only their outlines, hazed in misty lilac, visible."[18]

Along the way he sees signs "of man's restless advent and pioneer-age"—the dugout, the "scantling-hut," the telegraph pole, settlements

17. Platte Canyon, Colorado

of log houses, surveyors. "Once, a canvas office where you could send a message by electricity anywhere around the world!"[19]

Their train climbs to Kenosha Summit and Whitman and Reitzel look down on South Park, of "paradisiac loveliness." Mountain peaks "in every variety of perspective, every hue of vista, fringe the view." Whitman thinks: "Talk, I say again, of going to Europe, of visiting the ruins of feudal castles, or Coliseum remains, or kings' palaces—when you can come *here*."[20]

Both Geist and Martin sent their eastern readers lively accounts of their Leadville excursion. That Saturday Colonel Leonard Eicholtz, the chief construction engineer for the "South Park" (and a former Lancasterian), rode with them and explained the unusual methods required to build even a narrow-gauge railroad up the canyon of the Platte River, around "Muleshoe Curve" above Webster, and over the steep grades of Kenosha Pass.[21]

From Red Hill in South Park, Captain W. S. Tough, superintendent of the Denver and Leadville Despatch Line, using a two-horse open wagon, was their driver or "whip."[22] Martin thought Tough did his best to give the eastern newspapermen "a special show."[23] As Geist told it:

> Captain Tough has the reputation of being one of the most daring and skillful Jehus of the Rocky Mountains, and he fully sustained his reputation by driving us over the twenty-five miles in three hours and twenty-five minutes, and landing us in Leadville several hours ahead of the stages. He was very kind to the writer, who occupied the rear seat, in occasionally admonishing us in the language of Hank Smith, to "Keep your seat, Mr. Greeley!" as the vehicle bounced over the dust-hidden boulders at some precipitous curve with only a foot between us and fifteen hundred feet of almost perpendicular destruction on the left and a wall of snow-capped mountains on the right.[24]

Geist thought Leadville was "the greatest marvel of a marvelous country in a marvelous age." He was impressed by "the cuisine and appointments for comfort" of the Clarendon Hotel where they stayed. He noted the variety of structures in town, "from a brick opera house, now going up, the aristocratic seaside-style of cottage on 'Fifth Avenue,'

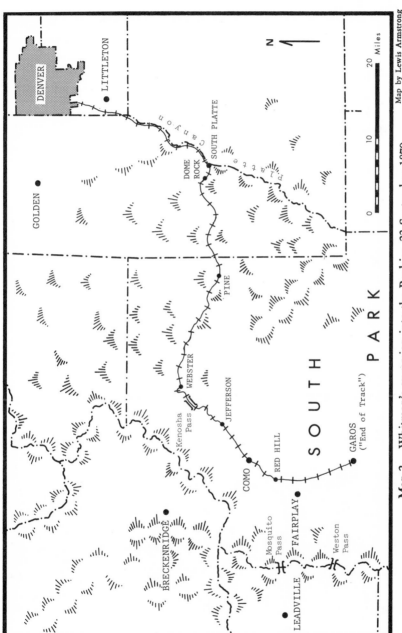

Map 2. Whitman's excursion into the Rockies, 22 September 1879

Map by Lewis Armstrong

down to the log-and-mud cabin and the 'dug-out' in the side of the hill." He also noted the well-stocked stores, the water system, and the just-completed gas works. "The town is all business and excitement," he wrote.[25]

Both journalists also wrote about the dark side of Leadville life, about the deadly "Leadville quartette" of Geist's description: "the metallic fumes of smelting furnaces, wholesale gambling, drinking whiskey, and prostitution."[26] "Sunday in Leadville," wrote Martin, is a "fete day" when one can see the town "in the pride of its wickedness." But he thought there were "harbingers" of civilization in the establishment of churches and in other slowly developing elements of law and order.[27]

Returning from Leadville at six in the morning on Monday, they were given "another John Gilpin ride," according to Geist. They reached Fairplay "with both seats broken down, the side of the wagon bursted out, and one of the buffers of the brakes 'dislocated.'" Geist did "volunteer service in going down the steep grades, by holding a piece of plank between the brake-clamp and the tire."[28]

They arrived at Red Hill well in advance of the train bringing up Whitman and Reitzel from Denver. At last reunited, the four men

18. South Park, viewed from Kenosha Summit

went sightseeing to the end of the track at Guiraud, twelve miles down the line. There they watched the stages arriving from over Weston Pass.[29] The *Specimen Days* jottings to the contrary, Guiraud (Garos), then, not Leadville, is at the ends of those lines Whitman drew on the maps for Burroughs and Gilchrist.

The poet and his friends got back to the American House at about ten o'clock that Monday evening.[30] We can imagine that what Geist and Martin endured going over Mosquito Pass and what they had observed of the "Leadville fever" figured large in their conversation at dinner that night.

6

THE PRAIRIE STATES

A newer garden of creation, no primal solitude,
Dense, joyous, modern, populous millions, cities and farms,
With iron interlaced, composite, tied, many in one,
By all the world contributed—freedom's and law's and thrift's
    society,
The crown and teeming paradise, so far, of time's accumulations,
To justify the past.

Leaves of Grass, 1881

Heading Eastward

In *Specimen Days* Whitman pretends that he "staid several days" in Denver after his return from the mountains.[1] In fact, he and his companions left Denver the next morning, Tuesday the twenty-third, taking the eight o'clock narrow-gauge Denver and Rio Grande Railway, then still part of the Santa Fe system.[2] Running south, they enjoyed the panorama of the Rockies which in the changing autumn sunlight seemed to Whitman "the most spiritual show of objective Nature I ever beheld." What he could see of Pike's Peak, however, disappointed him; he thought perhaps he had expected "something stunning."[3] "I was at Pike's Peak," he later wrote Peter Doyle.[4]

When the men were in Denver they had been impressed by how far they had traveled, and by the relatively shorter distance remaining to San Francisco. Undoubtedly they talked about the possibility of going farther west—but other plans and obligations at home (including the *New Era*'s libel suit) kept them from even stopping to visit the Garden of the Gods near Colorado Springs, much to Geist's regret.[5] Whitman wrote in his notebook: "I did not go to San Francisco, though I hope to do so one of these days. Indeed I have a good deal of travel laid out; (among the rest Tennessee and Alabama)."[6] In *Specimen Days* he changed this to regrets about not visiting Yellowstone National Park and, in the other direction, Veta Pass—"wanted to go over the Santa Fe trail away southwestward to New Mexico."[7]

At Pueblo the party turned east, boarding the Atchison, Topeka and Santa Fe Railroad, and had, or imagined they had, "whetting glimpse-tastes of . . . Bald Mountain, the Spanish peaks, Sangre de Christos, Mile-Shoe-curve (. . . 'the boss railroad curve of the universe') fort Garland . . . and the three great peaks of the Sierra Blancas." Following the Arkansas River eastward they again traveled through the plains, alternating "long sterile stretches" with "green, fertile and grassy" sections where they saw large herds of sheep.[8]

> We pass Fort Lyon—lots of adobie houses—limitless pasturage, appropriately fleck'd with . . . herds of cattle—in due time the declining sun in the west—a sky of limpid pearl over all—and so evening on the great plains. A calm, pensive, boundless landscape— the perpendicular rocks of the north Arkansas, hued in twilight—a thin line of violet on the southwestern horizon—the palpable coolness and slight aroma—a belated cow-boy with some unruly member of his herd—an emigrant wagon toiling yet a little further, the horses slow and tired—two men, apparently father and son, jogging along on foot—and around all the indescribable *chiaroscuro* and sentiment, (profounder than anything at sea), athwart these endless wilds.[9]

On this eastbound part of his journey Whitman saw again the yellow flower that had greeted him all along the way. He had seen it first days before when they were crossing Ohio, and had jotted down in his notebook: "Yellow flowers thick every where clear / light yellow. What are they?"[10] Crossing the plains on his way to Denver he had again noted "the yellow wild flowers."[11] By the time of writing *Specimen Days* he had identified the flower as "the coreopsis," with which he then claimed an old acquaintance in his walks around Timber Creek and on his wider travels in the East.[12]

At 4:50 on Wednesday morning, the twenty-fourth, the party got off at Sterling in central Kansas, and took a break (a day and a night) from train travel.[13] Whitman looked up Ed Lindsey, an "old-young soldier friend of mine of war times," now married and with a son, and "running the hotel" in Sterling.[14] Presumably, Whitman stayed at Lindsey's hotel, as did his companions, though the latter might have visited in private homes. Sterling, according to Geist, was a Lancaster settlement,[15] and they "enjoyed the hospitality of . . . big-hearted Lancaster friends there."[16]

That night Geist and Martin were guest speakers at a meeting of Republicans in a storeroom in the town's central block. According to the next-day's *Sterling Weekly Bulletin*, Martin "made some excellent points against the Greenback movement, and opened the eyes of many who were inclined toward that party."[17] However, the next-day's *Rice County Gazette*, also a Sterling weekly, thought that every position which Martin took against the Greenbackers "has been overturned time and time again by Greenback speakers and writers."[18]

Both papers also noted Whitman's presence in town. The *Gazette* reported "the old poet" as saying that "much as the grandeur of the mountains impressed him, the impression of the plains will remain longest with him." The paper added the hope that "Mr. Whitman will embody these impressions in some of his elegant poetry."[19]

The next morning, Thursday the twenty-fifth, the men made another early start, departing on the same 4:50 train. Whitman later wrote to Doyle that he had "hard work" getting away from Lindsey, who wanted him to stay the winter.[20]

We have Whitman's views of this part of the trip in *Specimen Days*:

> The sun up about half an hour; nothing can be fresher or more beautiful than this time, this region. I see quite a field of my yellow flower in full bloom. At intervals dots of nice two-story houses, as we ride swiftly by. Over the immense area, flat as a floor, visible for twenty miles in every direction in the clear air, a prevalence of autumn-drab and reddish-tawny herbage—sparse stacks of hay and enclosures, breaking the landscape—as we rumble by, flocks of prairie-hens starting up. Between Sterling and Florence a fine country.[21]

Around six that evening the party arrived at Kansas City where they were reunited with their railroad friends, Smart and Devereux.[22] This time they did go to the Coates House, the famed hotel operated by Geist's Lancaster friend, Kersey Coates.[23]

That Friday, the twenty-sixth, must have been a busy one for the men. Whitman tells us in *Specimen Days* that he visited a hog-packing plant.[24] Geist reported in the *New Era* that he explored the Missouri "flats" and visited an agricultural implement works belonging to friends from the East, and that Smart and Devereux took them to the

19. Coates House, Kansas City

Kansas City Industrial and Agricultural Exhibition, which was on its last day.[25] The *Kansas City Daily Times* reported that Whitman attended the horseraces there: "WALT WHITMAN, the famous American poet, tarried in Kansas City yesterday, on his return from Leadville. He took in (or rather was taken in by) the races, and fooled away an hour or two listening to the 'barbaric yawp' which ironically greeted the favorite as he passed under the wire, at the expense of the suckers in the pool box. It is safe to say MR. WHITMAN didn't contribute to the pool box nor indulge in any poetic gush over the Imposition."[26]

There are two other Kansas City "pictures" of Whitman. One has him in what we might judge to be an invented scene, sitting "leisurely in a store in Main street" and writing about the women he sees in the "streaming crowd" flowing by on the sidewalks:

> The ladies (and the same in Denver) are all fashionably drest, and have the look of "gentility" in face, manner and action, but they do *not* have, either in physique or the mentality appropriate to them, any high native originality of spirit or body, (as the men certainly have, appropriate to them.) They are "intellectual" and fashionable, but dyspeptic-looking and generally doll-like; their ambition evidently is to copy their eastern sisters. Something far different and in advance must appear, to tally and complete the superb masculinity of the West, and maintain and continue it.[27]

The other picture is of Whitman strolling down Main Street, the very figure of good health and well-being. That description appeared in the *Daily Times* on 28 September, two days after the poet's visit in Kansas City. It is probable that Whitman wrote it himself and left it behind as another press release:

> Walt Whitman is aging fast—he is in his sixtieth year—but those who had the pleasure of meeting him in Kansas City perceived that his mental vigor is unabated and he has been so much recuperated by his western trip that his herculean constitution may hold the enemy at bay for years to come. Tall and robust, six feet high, red face, profuse and uncut beard, long white hair, gait easy and slow, and weighing nearly 200 pounds, he looks outrageously healthy and till his paralytic stroke some years ago, prided himself on his perfect bodily condition, muscle and clean blood. He loafed along down Main street as leisurely as he would have done on Broadway or Pennsylvania avenue, and hundreds who saw his imposing figure, clad in English gray, with a wide, turned-over shirt collar open at the neck, and a drab plantation hat, would have eyed him still more curiously if told that the large, dispassionate, handsome, splendidly proportioned "animal," as he calls himself, was the clerk, farmer, carpenter, hospital nurse, and printer who wrote "Leaves of Grass," and put it into type with his own hands.[28]

20. Main Street, Kansas City, about 1879

That Friday evening the four men again boarded a St. Louis, Kansas City and Northern train and headed for St. Louis.[29] After another night in reclining coach seats they arrived in that city Saturday morning, the twenty-seventh. There, as Geist recited it, "[we] dropped our Poet to the care of his friends, and in twenty minutes were on our way home . . . , and arrived 'on time' in Lancaster on Sunday evening."[30]

7

WHAT BEST I SEE IN THEE
To U.S.G. return'd from his World's Tour

What best I see in thee,
Is not that where thou mov'st down history's great highways,
Ever undimm'd by time shoots warlike victory's dazzle,
Or that thou sat'st where Washington sat, ruling the land in peace,
Or thou the man whom feudal Europe feted, venerable Asia
    swarm'd upon,
Who walk'd with kings with even pace the round world's prome-
    nade;
But that in foreign lands, in all thy walks with kings,
Those prairie sovereigns of the West, Kansas, Missouri, Illinois,
Ohio's, Indiana's millions, comrades, farmers, soldiers, all to the
    front,
Invisibly with thee walking with kings with even pace the round
    world's promenade,
Were all so justified.

Leaves of Grass, 1881

St. Louis

When Whitman had stopped briefly in St. Louis two weeks earlier, he planned, as he told a reporter, to return for an "extended visit" with his brother and his nieces.[1] Geist, evidently, understood when they left the poet in St. Louis that he'd remain there "several weeks" and return to Camden late in October.[2] Close to his arrival, or shortly thereafter, Whitman became ill, but that, at the outset, did not alter his plans significantly, for on 11 October he wrote to Louisa that he expected to stay in St. Louis "perhaps two weeks longer," as he was "agreeably fixed here—& since I am so far, & shall probably never come again, I have concluded to stay awhile."[3] As it turned out, he lingered in St. Louis over three months, periodically announcing postponements of his departure date.[4]

It isn't definite when Whitman suffered what was apparently a physical relapse, because he wrote conflicting accounts of it to his friends. On 5 November he wrote to Peter Doyle that "three weeks ago" he was taken "sick & disabled, & hauled in here in St Louis for repairs," which would place the onset of his illness at about 15 October.[5] Five days after writing to Doyle, however, he wrote to Anne Gilchrist that he'd become ill "three weeks ago," which would be about 20 October.[6] More reliable probably than either of these tardy accounts is the earlier 11 October letter to Louisa in which he says he'd been "quite unwell" for "nine or ten days"—that is, since about the first of the month, just after his arrival.[7] This would be in accord with the note of general well-being sounded in his Kansas City press release.

73

21. Thomas Jefferson ("Jeff") Whitman

Whatever the degree of Whitman's illness, it was not the only factor in prolonging his stay. His desire, already noted, to visit with Jeff and his nieces, and his pleasure in "loafing" around St. Louis again were also factors, as was, possibly, toward the end, a need for money to make the rest of the trip home. And, though he undoubtedly had periods of illness in St. Louis, he was not mainly a house-bound invalid during his visit there.

Jeff's house at 2316 Pine Street, on a grid going west from the river (much like Philadelphia), was about twenty-three blocks from the levee, too far for Whitman to walk, probably, even on his best days. There were streetcars, however, and Jeff took him about in his carriage, quite likely taking him downtown with him when he went to his office in City Hall on Eleventh Street.[8] From there Whitman could walk farther downtown, stopping in, as he reports, at a drugstore on Fourth Street "partly to get a glass of Vichy & partly to sit down and rest myself, and most of all to see the oceanic crowd of humanity (in full currents) that rolled along."[9] St. Louis, he observed, "fuses northern and southern qualities, perhaps native and foreign ones, to perfection, rendezvous the whole stretch of the Mississippi and Missouri rivers, and its American electricity goes well with its German phlegm. Fourth, Fifth and Third streets are store-streets, showy, modern, metropolitan, with hurrying crowds, vehicles, horse-cars, hubbub, plenty of people, rich goods, plate-glass windows, iron fronts often five and six stories high."[10] There were, however, two things, he wrote Louisa, "you & I w'd never get used to, & would spoil all, that is the air you breathe is always tainted with coal smoke & pungent gas—& a perpetual dust & smut & little black motes, that forever smut your clothes & hands & face, all the time, night & day."[11]

Whitman went "most every day," he wrote Burroughs, to the public library, by which he meant the Mercantile Library on Fifth Street. There, through the courtesy of John Napier Dyer, the librarian, he read the New York and Philadelphia papers.[12] That fall he made the acquaintance of William Torrey Harris and of Henry C. Brokmeyer, leading figures in the St. Louis Movement, a group of "toploftical Hegelian transcendentalists," as Whitman described them in a letter to Burroughs.[13] Harris was the editor of the *Journal of Speculative Philosophy*, the October issue of which he gave to Whitman; he was also superintendent of schools in St. Louis. In thanking him for the copy of the journal and for some other materials he had sent, Whitman indicated that he'd like "to spend an hour in one of your public schools."[14] Subsequently Whitman apparently made fairly regular visits to a kindergarten, perhaps in the Eliot Branch School at Fifteenth and Pine, or in the Franklin School at Eighteenth and Lucas, both fairly near Jeff's house.[15] There he entertained the children with stories, including the fable of the two cats who take the same trip; but whereas one returns to tell of wonders discovered, the other reports only horrors encountered. It was, Whitman explained to Horace Traubel years later, a story of two habits of mind.[16]

Going west earlier in the month Geist had marveled at the Eads Bridge, completed five years before. That "great iron artery," he wrote, was "the most daring and wonderful piece of engineering now completed in the country."[17] Whitman was no less taken by the structure. He sent pictures of it to Doyle ("one of my favorite sights"),[18] and to Burroughs ("where I have loafed many hours. . . . I dont believe there can be a grander thing of the kind on earth").[19] In *Specimen Days* he

22. Mercantile Library, St. Louis, about 1880

dates "Oct. 29th, 30th, and 31st" this description of a night visit to the bridge:

> Wonderfully fine, with the full harvest moon, dazzling and silvery. I have haunted the river every night lately, where I could get a look at the bridge by moonlight. It is indeed a structure of perfection and beauty unsurpassable, and I never tire of it. The river at present is very low; I noticed to-day it had much more of a blue-clear look than usual. I hear the slight ripples, the air is fresh and cool, and the view, up or down, wonderfully clear, in the moonlight. I am out pretty late: it is so fascinating, dreamy. The cool night-air, all the influences, the silence, with those far-off eternal stars, do me good. I have been quite ill of late. And so, well-near the centre of our national demesne, these night views of the Mississippi.[20]

It testifies to the importance of the bridge to Whitman that in his traveling notebook for 27 November he recorded again, simply: "on St L Bridge."[21]

Other events that Whitman recorded of his St. Louis stay were a tour of Anheuser's brewery, on 22 November; a visit two days later by Joe Hall, a "Leadvillean" he had met in Colorado, perhaps on the "South Park"; and, earlier that month, on the sixth, an excursion to Crystal City to tour the plate-glass works there.[22] In *November Boughs*, where he describes the trip, he again makes it sound as though he had gone alone: "I went down that way to-day by the Iron Mountain Railroad—was switch'd off on a side-track four miles through woods and ravines, to Swash Creek, so-call'd, and there found Crystal City, and immense Glass Works, built (and evidently built to stay) right in the pleasant rolling forest."[23] In fact, Whitman was one of a rather large "select company," as the *St. Louis Daily Globe-Democrat* reported, to make "the merry junketing party." According to that newspaper, James Green, a stockholder in the plate-glass company, invited a number of people to go by special train to visit the plant thirty-three miles to the south. In the party, besides Mr. and Mrs. Green, were the mayor and his secretary, Water Commissioner Whitman, "Walt Whitman, the poet," the street commissioner, a judge, eleven other prominent St. Louis and Carondelet men (two of them with their wives), the secretary of the company, and some press people.[24]

23. Eads Bridge, St. Louis, about 1874

At Crystal Station their private car was detached and taken by a branch line to Crystal City. There the party was escorted to the plant where the general manager, George F. Neale, formerly manager of a glass works in England, led them on an inspection tour. Whitman was most impressed by "the melting in the pots (a wondrous process, a real poem)," as he wrote:

> —saw the molten stuff (a great mass of a glowing pale yellow color) taken out of the furnaces (I shall never forget that Pot, shape, color, concomitants, more beautiful than any antique statue,) pass'd into the adjoining casting-room, lifted by powerful machinery, pour'd out on its bed (all glowing, a newer, vaster study for colorists, indescribable, a pale red-tinged yellow, of tarry consistence, all lambent,) roll'd by a heavy roller into rough plate glass, I should

78

say ten feet by fourteen, then rapidly shov'd into the annealing oven, which stood ready for it.²⁵

After the tour through the plant the ladies accompanied Mrs. Neale to the manager's residence, and the men went to the City Hall. There they smoked "fragrant Havanas" and listened to the employees' brass band. Someone asked Walt to recite one of his poems. He declined by saying, "This day has been a poem to me; it has been a pleasant jaunt and should suffice for all." At about two o'clock the whole party had dinner, "a demnition fine spread," according to one reporter. Then the Neales accompanied their visitors back to Crystal Station.²⁶

Returning to St. Louis at sundown, Whitman had another good view of the Mississippi River, of steamboats going downstream, and of Mars glistening in the sky over Illinois. Then, approaching the city in the early night, he was struck by the colorful sight:

.... I saw some (to me) novel effects in the zinc smelting establishments, the tall chimneys belching flames at the top, while inside through the openings at the façades of the great tanks burst forth (in regular position) hundreds of fierce tufts of a peculiar blue (or green) flame, of a purity and intensity, like electric lights—illuminating not only the great buildings themselves, but far and near outside, like hues of the aurora borealis, only more vivid. (So that— remembering the Pot from the crystal furnace—my jaunt seem'd to give me new revelations in the color line.)²⁷

In addition to his visiting and sightseeing in and around St. Louis, Whitman kept busy with a steady and extensive personal and business correspondence, and with keeping the records of his bookselling business. He had Louisa mail him what letters had accumulated in Camden, and so brought himself up-to-date in his correspondence. He wrote about two dozen business letters in this St. Louis period, in addition to a half-dozen requests to Louisa to send out books in response to orders he received. On the personal side, besides letters to Louisa and George, he wrote often to his sisters—six times to Hannah Heyde, and four times to Mary Van Nostrand. To them, to Lou and George, to Crosby S. Noyes, editor of the *Washington* (D.C.) *Evening Star*, and, as we have seen, to John Burroughs and Anne Gilchrist, he sent maps of his journey. All in all, Whitman wrote over fifty letters or postcards during his three-months' stay in St. Louis.[28]

Writing for publication was more difficult. Two one-paragraph sections of *Specimen Days*, "The Silent General," a comment on Grant, dated 28 September, and "President Hayes' Speeches," dated 30 September, appear, if we trust Whitman's dates, to have been originally drafted just after his arrival in St. Louis (the Grant item the next day, in fact).[29] But this is the probable period of his relapse, so we might question the accuracy of the dating.

In the Grant piece Whitman writes that the former president "landed in San Francisco yesterday" on his round-the-world tour, which, according to Whitman's dating, would be 27 September. The fact is that Grant arrived in San Francisco on 20 September, a whole week earlier.[30] Similarly, in the Hayes item, Whitman says, "I see President Hayes has come out West," which suggests his noting that Hayes has in recent days started a tour of the West. Again, Hayes started his tour in mid-September, at the time of the Kansas Silver Wedding.[31] He had been invited to attend the Old Settlers' meeting, but wrote to them that he couldn't get to Kansas until later. As his tour turned out, he finally got to Lawrence on 27 September;[32] on the thirtieth, the date of Whitman's paragraph, he was in Springfield, Illinois, and heading east on the final lap of his tour.[33]

The Grant piece has "Kansas City" crossed out in the upper left corner, and is written on letterhead stationery from Jeff's office. Floyd Stovall, in his note on the editing of this item, suggests that Whitman may have drafted it in Kansas City on his return from Denver, and on paper he had acquired from Jeff's office when he was going west two months before.[34] The Hayes piece, Stovall suggests, may have been developed from notes made in Kansas City, and added to in St. Louis or, possibly, in Camden later.[35] Another possible explanation of the composition of these two items is that Whitman wrote them both in Denver on Sunday, 21 September, the day after Grant's return to the United States, and that he revised them and roughly dated them in Camden in 1882 when he was reworking his materials for *Specimen Days*. The two items, along with the preceding section, "The Women of the West," appear to constitute a transitional "Kansas City" sequence in *Specimen Days*. At the conclusion of the Hayes piece Whitman adds, "From Kansas City I went to St. Louis," apparently forgetting that, in arranging the order of these materials, he had already moved on to St. Louis in at least two preceding sections, "Mississippi Valley Literature" and "An Interviewer's Item" (which is accurately dated 17 October; curiously, it is placed ahead of his supposedly later September items).[36]

The earlier composition of the Grant and Hayes pieces is further supported by Whitman's 11 October letter to Louisa in which he says of his St. Louis stay, "I have not written any thing for publication yet here, as I have not felt well, but I want to, before I leave, as this trip is a great revelation, especially the Colorado journey, & the mountains—."[37]

One poem, foreshadowed in the prose piece on Grant (and in the speech intended for the Old Settlers, and in the Denver "interview"), is definitely from the St. Louis days. That is the salute to Grant, "What Best I See in Thee," which he mailed off to the *Philadelphia Press* on 9 December.[38] Taken, apparently, as drum-beating for the "Grant boom," the poem was satirized by the Democratic *New York Star*. As republished in the *Camden Daily Post*, the *Star*'s way of having fun with Whitman's lines was to present the poem as prose and to provide a "glossary" of several explanatory notes, thus:

What Best I See in Thee

(Gen. Grant in Philadelphia, Dec. ...., '79)

What best I see in thee, is not that where thou mov'st* down history's great highways ever undimmed by time shoots† warlike victory's dazzle‡; or that thou sat'st where Washington, Lincoln sat, ruling the land in peace; or then the man whom feudal Europe feted, §venerable Asia swarm'd upon; who walk'd with kings with even pace the round world's promenade; but that in war and peace, and in thy walks with kings,** these average prairie sovereigns of the West, Kansas, Missouri, Illinois,†† Ohio's, Indiana's millions, comrades, O farmers, soldiers, all to the front, invisibly with thee walking with kings with even pace the 4-14-44 round world's promenade. ‡‡Were all so justified?
Walt Whitman
§§St Louis, Dec 16

    * MOV'ST—Tramp

    † SHOOTS—Slang term applied to hats (its application to dazzle a happy idea of the poet.)

    ‡ DAZZLE—As here used probably has some connection with Blizzard

    § "VENERABLE ASIA SWARM'D UPON"—An entomological allusion

    ** "WALKED WITH KINGS"—a slang expression in the game of poker

    †† AVERAGE PRAIRIE SOVEREIGNS—Suckers

    O COMR Des-Pard [sic]

    4-11-44 [sic] "ROUND WORLD'S PROMENADE"—Swing'ng round the circle

    ‡‡ "WERE ALL SO JUSTIFIED"—an expression used by printers

    §§ St. LOUIS—The name of a small Western village[39]

During his prolonged visit in St. Louis, Whitman also spent some of his time, as usual, attending to the press. We may read a 17 October *St. Louis Post-Dispatch* "interview," a brief, edited part of which is in *Specimen Days*, as another press release.[40] It appeared in the *Post-Dispatch* as follows:

> Walt Whitman, the poet, is visiting his brother at 2316 Pine street, in this city, resting after his trip to Kansas, and recovering from an attack of sickness. Mr. Whitman is a very remarkable looking man. His long, snow-white hair flows down and mingles with his fleecy beard, giving him a venerable expression, which his grave eyes and well-marked features confirm. Whitman impresses one at once as being a sage, and his thoughtful, original speech confirms the idea.
>
> A *Post-Dispatch* reporter called on the author of "Leaves of Grass" this morning, and after a somewhat desultory conversation abruptly asked him:
>
> "Do you think we are to have a distinctively American literature?"
>
> "It seems to me," said he, "that our work at present, and for a long time to come, is to lay the materialistic foundations of a great nation, in products, in commerce, in vast networks of inter-communication, and in all that relates to the comforts and supplies of vast masses of men and families, on a very grand scale, and those with

freedom of speech and ecclesiasticism. This we have founded and are carrying out on a grander scale than ever hitherto, and it seems to me that those great central States from Ohio to Colorado, and from Lake Superior down to Tennessee, the prairie States, will be the theater of our great future. Ohio, Illinois, Indiana, Missouri, Kansas and Colorado seem to me to be the seat and field of these very ideas. They seem to be carrying them out."

"Materialistic prosperity in all its varied forms and on the grand scale of our times, with those other points that I mentioned, inter-communication and freedom, are first to be attended to. When those have their results and get settled then a literature worthy of us will begin to be defined from our nebulous conditions. Although we have elegant and finished writers, none of them express America or her spirit in any respect whatever."

"What will be the character of the American literature when it does form?"

"Do you know that I have thought of that vaguely often, but have never before been asked the question. It will be something entirely new, entirely different. As we are a new nation with almost a new geography, and a new spirit, the expression of them will have to be new. In form, in combination we shall take the same old font of type, but what we set up will never have been set up before. It will be the same old font that Homer and Shakspeare used, but our use will be new."

"Modern poetry and art run to a sweetness and refinement which are really foreign to us, they are not ours. Everywhere as I went through the Rocky Mountains, three weeks ago, especially the Platte Canon, I said to myself, 'Here are my poems, not finished temples, not graceful architecture, but great naturalness and rugged power—primitive nature.'"

"My idea of one great feature of future American poetry is the expression of comradeship. That is a main point with me. Then breadth, moderness and consistency with science."

"Poetry, as yet given to us even by our own bards, is essentially feudal and antique. Our greatest man is Emerson. Bryant, I think, has a few pulsations. Whittier is a puritan poet without unction— without juice. I hardly know what to say about Longfellow. The best promise in America of those things is in a certain range of young men that are coming on the stage, that are yet voiceless. They are appearing in the Eastern cities and in the West. They have not yet begun to speak because the magazines and publishing houses are in the hands of the fossils."

"There is a great underlying strata of young men and women who cannot speak because the magazines are in the hands of old fogies like Holland or fops like Howells. They are like water dammed up. They will burst forth some day. They are very American. Emerson is our first man. He is in every way what he should be. He is a rounded, finished man, complete in himself. Our living Bancroft and our dead Ticknor I think first-class men."

"What do you think of Bret Harte?"

"He is smart, facile and witty in the old sense. What a miserable business it is to take out of this great outgrowth of Western character, which is something more heroic than ever the old poets wrote about, to have taken out only a few ruffians and delerium tremens specimens, and made them the representatives of California personality. An artist would have taken the heroic personalities, but Bret Harte and the persons who followed him have taken these characters and made them stand for the whole. I think it is an outrage. He seems to me to have taken Dickens' treatment of the slums of London and transferred it to California."

"I think Tennyson the leading man in modern poetry. Nobody has expressed like Tennyson the blending of the most perfect verbal melody with the heart sickness of modern times."

"He has caught that undertone of ennui in a way that will last while men read. I myself have been ambitious to do something entirely different from that, while I can appreciate him. The whole tendency of poetry has been toward refinement. I have felt that was not worthy of America. Something more vigorous, *al fresco*, was needed, and then more than all I determined from the beginning to put a whole living man in the expression of a poem, without wincing. I thought the time had come to do so, and I thought America was the place to do it. Curious as it may appear, it had never yet been done. An entire human being physically, emotionally, and in his moral and spiritual nature. And also to express what seems to me had been left unexpressed, our own country and our own times. I have come now a couple of thousand miles, and the greatest thing to me in this Western country is the realization of my 'Leaves of Grass.' It tickles me hugely to find how thoroughly it and I have been in rapport. How my poems have defined them. I have really had their spirit in every page without knowing. I had made Western people talk to me, but I never knew how thoroughly a Western man I was till now."

"And how about religion?"

"I could only say that, as she develops, America will be a thoroughly religious nation. Toleration will grow, and the technique of religion, sectarianism, will more and more give out."

"Politically?"

"Politically, as far as I can see, we have established ourselves. The basis has been all right. We have nothing to do de novo. I think the theory and practice of American government, without its National and State governments, are stable. It seems to be established without danger, without end."

"And how about Canada?"

"I think Canada and Cuba and Mexico will gravitate to us. We could take the whole world in if it was fit for it, which it is not. There is no danger in enlargement. We can take in all the country from the isthmus to the North pole. Instead of endangering us it will only balance us, give us a greater area of base."

"Our American greatness and vitality are in the bulk of our people, not in a gentry like the old world. The greatness of our army was in the rank and file, and so with the nation. Other nations had their vitality in a few, a class, but we have it in the bulk of the people. Our leading men are not of much account and never have been, but the average of the people is immense, beyond all history."

"Lincoln seems to me our greatest specimen personality. Sometimes I think that in all departments, literature and art included, that will be the way our greatness will exhibit itself. We will not have great individuals or great leaders, but a great bulk, unprecedentedly great."[41]

Robert Underwood Johnson, then on the editorial staff of *Century Magazine*, wrote to Whitman to inquire which younger writers he thought were being neglected. Whitman responded that he had no names because he "spoke mainly of a class, or rather a leaven & spirit—."[42] He included a pasted-up, slightly revised version of the "interview" with the suggestion that Johnson might try to place it in a New York publication.[43]

Another obvious press release written in this period is "A Poet's Western Visit," which appeared in the *Washington* (D.C.) *Evening*

Star of 15 November, and in the *St. Louis Globe-Democrat* the following week:

Walt Whitman is still in St. Louis, after spending the last three months among the Rocky Mountains and the great plains of Kansas and Colorado. After returning to the Atlantic States, he intends traveling and lecturing at intervals, as his strength permits, being yet a half paralytic. Healthy to perfection for over fifty years, he commenced in 1862, as many of our readers know, those practical missionary labors in the war hospitals and in front, and continued them on to 1866, in the thickest of that time and amid all its turmoils and suspense, night and day with his own hands nursing alike both Union and rebel soldiers whenever they fell in his way.

The poet is now in his sixty-first year. Though crippled and paralyzed, and quite ill some time here in St. Louis, but now recovering, his spirits are unbroken, and he looks in good flesh, living largely in the open air, and occasionally traveling. He was in New York and on Long Island all the early summer. He continues to write at times. He has quite ready for publication a little prose book, characteristic notes of outdoor observations, especially of the woods, fields, and seaside, interspersed with reminiscences and criticism, and including this late Rocky Mountain and prairie jaunt, all told in his own way, by impromptu memoranda of the spot and time. His permanent residence is in Camden, New Jersey. He publishes and sells his books himself. He is understood as desiring engagements to lecture and read his poems the coming winter. He returns East this month, after a Western trip to and fro of 5,000 miles. He is stopping in the city at the house of his brother, Water Commissioner Whitman.

Mr. Whitman says no one can begin to know what America is, or what it is destined to be in the near future, without exploring and living awhile in Ohio, Indiana, Illinois, Missouri, Kansas and Colorado. He is in love with the last three especially. But all these vast prairie States are laid out for the home of humanity, on the largest democratic scale. Wondrous rivers, railroads everywhere, plenty of wood, interminable and fertile meadows, wheat, fruit, exhaustless gold and silver, coal and iron, indeed every mineral, every agricultural product, absolutely without limit, and every manufacture known. Then such a prolific region, everywhere swarms of vigorous children. It is already the hospitable resort of the globe. But the babe is born, the poet prophesies, that will see this area the home of 100,000,000 of human beings, and the real and ideal America of the future.[44]

The reference to the "little prose book" that was "quite ready" is one of several such "advertisements" in the newspaper reports of this period. Geist, for instance, reported as early as 30 September that Whitman was preparing "a pastoral on the life and manners and wonderful enterprise of the people of the great West."[45] About a month later he told his readers that Whitman "has nearly ready for publication a volume of prose containing notes of his recent jaunt in the Rocky Mountains."[46] On 1 December the *Camden Daily Post* reported in similar terms that Whitman "has ready for publication a volume of prose, containing outdoor notes of his recent jaunt among the Rocky Mountains."[47]

However premature these reports turned out to be, they affirm, as do the records of his correspondence and bookkeeping, that Whitman was forward-looking and active during much of his St. Louis visit. There were undoubtedly some very bad days when he might have thought of himself again as a "batter'd, wreck'd old man," another Columbus "far, far from home." But in the three-month period, more typical, the record shows, were the days of further adventuring.

8

After reading the pages of *Specimen Days* do you object that they are a great jumble, everything scattered, disjointed, bound together without coherence, without order or system? My answer would be, So much the better do they reflect the life they are intended to stand for.

Though I would not have dared to gather the various pieces of the following book in a single volume with a generic name unless I felt the strong inward thread of spinality running through all the pieces and giving them affinity-purpose—I yet realize that the collection is indeed a melange and its cohesion and singleness of purpose not so evident at first glance.

"Autobiographical Notes," 1882

Back in Camden

Whitman wrote to John Burroughs on 23 November that he would probably leave St. Louis after another ten days, "but I am not fixed," he added.[1] Actually, it would be another six weeks before he would get away. Burroughs's next letter to him, on 29 December, contained a hundred-dollar "Christmas Remembrance" from an unnamed donor (James T. Fields). Whitman may have thought the money was from R. M. Bucke who had in early November offered him that same amount as a gift or as a loan, an offer he had rejected. On this later occasion he accepted the money gratefully, writing to Burroughs on January 2: "Believe me, I feel the gift, & it comes just right too."[2] Whether he actually needed the money to get back to Camden remains a question. Forney's railroad passes had been for himself and friends "from Philadelphia to St. Louis and back."[3] Since he was no longer with Forney he probably had to pay his own way, as had the others, for the last leg of the homeward trip. That weekend, at any rate, he began preparations to leave Jeff's house. He departed St. Louis on Sunday morning at eight o'clock, 4 January.[4]

The backtracking journey home, though largely over the same rail routes he had taken going west, must have contrasted bleakly with the trip four months earlier when he was one of the "referees'" for a companionable group. Another difference was that this time the stretch east of Pittsburgh was by daylight. He took in the sights, jotting down notes on the passing scenes:

through Pensylvania [sic] / Jan 5 '80 [strikeover] by the RR / from Pittsburgh to / Altoonah, Harrisburgh [sic] / the fertile broken country, / the mining & coal interests / every where — the ? [sic] / — the beautiful-Conema and the Juniata river / — Altoonah — the [rocky crossed out] / [& crossed out] wooded & rocky / land, so healthy & / pure-air'd, with creeks / or ragged threads of / rivulets every where / — the perpetual clusters / of houses in shelter'd / places, along the mountains[5]

Another set of jottings:

— the paths, fences, / [two strikeovers] orchards — at long / intervals, a grave yard / — horse-shoe curve / — school houses not so / plenty, as far west — / — some of the mountain / scenery. [strikeover] very bold and / [strikeover] / — Pennsylvania / [state crossed out] land of amplitude and / varied industries / land of mountains and / health & pure air / — land of coal & iron / & railroads[6]

Whitman's train arrived in West Philadelphia at 7:20 Monday evening, 5 January.[7] Soon he was back in his other brother's house in Camden. That Wednesday the *Camden Daily Post* had a front-page story headlined "Walt Whitman Home Again." It was probably written by the poet himself:

After an absence since last August [sic] Walt Whitman returned yesterday [sic] to his home in Camden, from a long and varied journey through the Central States of the Union. His travel has been mainly devoted to Colorado, Kansas and Missouri, but he has made visits to four or five other states. His objects of especial attention have been the Rocky Mountains, the Great Plains, and the Mississippi River, with their life, scenery and idiosyncrasies. Of the West generally he says not the half has been told. He is in love with Denver City, and speaks admiringly of Missouri and Indiana.

Going and coming, largely by different routes with side excursions, Mr. Whitman has travelled over 5000 miles, and considers the trip the most valuable revelation of his life. He has not yet written out his impressions and notes, but will soon do so. After some pretty rugged experiences, and a tedious fit of sickness, he returns to Camden in his average health, and with strength and spirits "good enough to be mighty thankful for," as he expresses it.[8]

Despite the "tedious fit of sickness" in St. Louis, the over-all trip was greatly rewarding to Whitman. Something of his pleasure in it may be inferred from his already-noted sending of maps, school-boy fashion, showing John Burroughs, Anne Gilchrist, and the others how far west he had traveled. The jaunt bolstered his self-esteem. He had gone west first-class, and had been treated as a distinguished visitor at Bismarck Grove and in several cities.

The publicity helped too. The interviews, real and contrived; the numerous descriptions of "the venerable poet" with his open collar; the reports of his wanderings—"Walt Whitman is doing the Rocky Mountains"; the reported plans for a new book—all this in Forney's *Progress*, in the *Philadelphia Press*, in Geist's *New Era*, and in several other papers—all this, part genuine reportage, part self-advertisement, undoubtedly helped Whitman's book sales the next year. As Edwin Haviland Miller has shown (with Whitman's bank book as evidence), the poet in 1880 "sold his books with more success than he had experienced since 1876," and "turned himself about economically."[9]

The western jaunt produced little new poetry immediately identifiable with it. His "Spirit That Form'd This Scene," "The Prairie States," "Italian Music in Dakota," and "What Best I See in Thee" are the chief poetic expressions of the experience. But, as Gay Wilson Allen has observed, the trip confirmed a sense of the West he had already explored in his poetry.[10] He thought himself that the images of the West "tallied" with his imaginings, and he was pleased to see "how truthfully he had represented in his poetry the vastness, the life, the soil and the rankness of the West."[11]

And, much as Whitman's western experience put him directly in touch with a portion of his poetic catalogs, so also it drew him into a dramatic historical context again. The Silver Wedding at Bismarck Grove invoked Free Soil and the even larger movement of westward expansion—a "passage to India." And though the frontier was gone, the West was abuilding via the railroads, and he had for a time been witness to all that:

> "Always, after supper, take a walk half a mile long," says an old proverb, dryly adding, "and if convenient let it be upon your own land." I wonder does any other nation but ours afford opportunity for such a jaunt as this? Indeed has any previous period afforded it? No one, I discover, begins to know the real geographic,

democratic, indissoluble American Union in the present, or suspect it in the future, until he explores these Central States, and dwells awhile observantly on their prairies, or amid their busy towns, and the mighty father of waters. A ride of two or three thousand miles, "on one's own land," with hardly a disconnection, could certainly be had in no other place than the United States, and at no period before this. If you want to see what the railroad is, and how civilization and progress date from it—how it is the conqueror of crude nature, which it turns to man's use, both on small scales and on the largest—come hither to inland America.[12]

Though the jaunt yielded only a few poems, it did, of course, provide material for his projected book of prose. On his return home he was, as his last note on the trip has it, "Stored with exhaustless recollections."[13] With those recollections and with daybook jottings and other notes, he now had a whole new set of American materials for his next book.

In "A Happy Hour's Command," the opening section of *Specimen Days*, the poet tells us that on 2 July 1882, "down in the woods" on a fine day, he heard within the call to begin work to make a book out of his "huddle of diary-jottings, war-memoranda of 1862–'65, Nature-notes of 1877–'81, with Western and Canadian observations afterwards, all bundled up and tied by a big string."[14] That very hour he sensed the command, he said,

> —to go home, untie the bundle, reel out diary-scraps and memo-randa, just as they are, large or small, one after another, into print-pages, and let the melange's lackings and wants of connection take care of themselves. It will illustrate one phase of humanity anyhow; how few of life's days and hours (and they not by relative value or proportion, but by chance) are ever noted. Probably another point too, how we give long preparations for some object, planning and delving and fashioning, and then, when the actual hour of doing arrives, find ourselves still quite unprepared, and tumble the thing together, letting hurry and crudeness tell the story better than fine work. At any rate I obey my happy hour's command, which seems curiously imperative. May-be, if I don't do anything else, I shall send out the most wayward, spontaneous, fragmentary book ever printed.[15]

Whitman's "happy hour's command" in July is, of course, a fiction. It is true that on 20 June he had written to Rees Welsh, his publisher, that *Specimen Days and Thoughts* (as it was at first titled) was "mostly in MS."[16] But as early as 21 March he had written to Osgood, his previous publisher, that the book was "about got into shape."[17] By 19 July he had "made a start" getting the work to the printers, and by 23 July was reading first page proofs.[18] In other words, though he may have earlier put aside work on a book he had perhaps planned during his St. Louis stay (or even before, recalling his letter to Anne Gilchrist about a small book of nature jottings), his return to that work was a much more calculated step than the "command" in the woods reveals.

And there is authorial pretense, surely, in Whitman's statement that he would "reel out" his materials "just as they are, large or small, one after another, into print-pages, and let the melange's lackings and wants of connection take care of themselves." The waywardness in the western sections of *Specimen Days* derives not from such spontaneity but from Whitman's attempt to reconstruct his "diary-scraps and memoranda." In that attempt he was not always a good editor, as when he gives Topeka as the site of the Old Settlers' meeting, or when he misdates the Grant paragraph, or lets stand such an incongruity as "now, and from what I have seen and learn'd since."[19]

The other deliberate care that Whitman gave his western materials was to shape them to fit an almost fictional version of the trip that would enhance his reputation. Hence the suggestion of traveling alone, another Bayard Taylor roaming the storied West, and the omission of all references to the special hospitality and services he received by virtue of the status of his companions. Hence the carefully prepared "impromptu lines" and "hastily pencill'd" speeches and the as carefully placed "interviews."

In Whitman's revamping of his notes we see other pretenses—of visiting Leadville, of spending several days exploring Denver *after* a day's excursion in the mountains, and of having an old "floricultural friend," the coreopsis, follow him "from Barnegat to Pike's Peak." And, appropriate to the character he wishes to project (a persona, practically), he reports mainly in this section the smiling aspects of western American life. Of the two cats who took the same walk in his fable for the St. Louis school-children, he is the cat whose habit of mind was to report the wonderful. For what there was of the "grim" and the unpleasant, we need to consult his daybook and his letters.[20]

Writing about Bucke's biography of Whitman, published in 1883, the year after *Specimen Days*, Gay Wilson Allen notes that Whitman admitted he wrote the sketch in the book of his ancestry and early life. Allen then observes the "several glaring inaccuracies" in the sketch:

> For example, Whitman was said to have spent a whole year in New Orleans (actually only two months), and in an introductory chronological table (which may or may not have been written by Whitman) this was given as having taken place in 1848–1849. In general the poet's travels and his knowledge of American life were exaggerated, and much of his journalistic experience passed over in silence. His editorship of the Brooklyn *Times* was not mentioned at all, or his earlier editing of New York papers. It is difficult to understand how Whitman's memory could have tricked him so egregiously about the New Orleans sojourn, but the omissions could easily have been accidental. Probably Whitman wrote this sketch in haste, without attempting to verify the facts; yet it is difficult not to suspect that he deliberately stretched the period of his stay in the deep South. This may be a minor detail, but it shows that the poet was willing to make some adjustments in the facts in order to present his biography as he wished it to be.[21]

"Adjustments in the facts" are as evident in Whitman's account of his western jaunt as in his account of his southern one. So too are the errors he acknowledges as probable in his rushing copy to the printer that hot summer of 1882. The attempt here, then, has been to restore certain particulars to the record of his historic trip so that we might understand even better the "authentic glints, specimen-days" of a great poet's life.[22]

Notes

PREFACE

1. Robert Scholnick, "The Selling of the 'Author's Edition': Whitman, O'Connor, and the *West Jersey Press* Affair," *Walt Whitman Review* 23 (March 1977): 3–23.

CHAPTER 1

1. R. M. Bucke, *Walt Whitman* (Philadelphia: David McKay, 1883), p. 136.

2. The phrase, written this way, is Whitman's, and appears frequently in press reports of his trip. He calls himself this in *Specimen Days*; see *Prose Works 1892*, ed. Floyd Stovall (New York: New York University Press, 1963), I, "An Interregnum Paragraph," p. 119. See also his letter to Anne Gilchrist proposing a small book with the title *Idle Days and Nights of a half-Paralytic*. Mrs. Gilchrist responded with the hope that he would reconsider the title to leave out the "half-Paralytic," because she said, "health and vigour . . . must remain synonymous with our Walt's name." Walt Whitman, *The Correspondence*, ed. Edwin Haviland Miller (New York: New York University Press, 1964), III, letter #931, to Anne Gilchrist, 18 August 1879, p. 161. The Gilchrist response, dated 6 October 1879, is in Clara Barrus, *Whitman and Burroughs—Comrades* (1931; rpt. Port Washington, New York: Kennikat Press, 1968), pp. 147–148.

3. *Specimen Days*, p. 206.

4. *Progress*, 19 July 1879, p. 701.

5. R[oy] F. N[ichols], "Forney, John Wien," *DAB* (1931). Forney's own account of the election of Banks to the speakership is in his *Anecdotes of Public Men* (1873; rpt. New York: Da Capo Press, 1970), I, pp. 109–111, 373–382.

6. Frank Luther Mott, *American Journalism* (New York: The Macmillan Company, 1949), p. 347.

7. *Progress*, 19 July 1879, p. 701. George A. Crawford had been elected governor of Kansas in 1861, but had never served as chief executive because the Kansas Supreme Court ruled the election was held a year too early and was therefore illegal. See William E. Connelley, *A Standard History of Kansas and Kansans* (Chicago: Lewis Publishing Co., 1918), III, p. 1247. The Pennsylvanians regularly referred to him as "Governor" or "ex-Governor," perhaps confusing him with Samuel J. Crawford, no relation, who was Kansas's Republican governor from 1865 to 1868. Forney and George A. Crawford were undoubtedly acquainted through the commission for the 1876 International Exhibition (the Philadelphia centennial celebration) on which they both served, Crawford as the Kansas representative.

8. *Progress*, 13 September 1879, p. 879.

9. *St. Louis Daily Globe-Democrat*, 13 September 1879, p. 6. In 1867 Jeff had left an engineering position at the Brooklyn Water Works to go to St. Louis to construct and supervise a new water system there. His wife, Martha ("Mattie"), died there in 1873, leaving him with two daughters, Mannahatta and Jessie, who were nineteen and sixteen years old, respectively, when Whitman visited them in 1879. See *Mattie: The Letters of Martha Mitchell Whitman*, ed. Randall H. Waldron (New York: New York University Press, 1977), Introduction, pp. 1–26.

10. Walt Whitman, *Daybooks and Notebooks*, ed. William White (New York: New York University Press, 1978), I, *Daybooks, 1876–November 1881*, pp. 150–153.

11. *Progress*, 9 August 1879, p. 763.

12. Ibid., 19 July 1879, p. 701.

13. *Lancaster* (Pennsylvania) *Daily New Era*, 21 July 1879, p. 1.

14. Ibid. This account explains Whitman's daybook entries for 25 June and 19 July 1879, including "Stokely," the name of the police tug, and a clipping of fifty-three names, all of participants in the send-off. See *Daybooks, 1876–November 1881*, pp. 148, 150; and my article, "Whitman's *Daybooks*: Further Identifications," *Walt Whitman Review* 26 (June 1980): 72–74.

15. *Daily New Era*, 21 July 1879, p. 1.

16. Franklin Ellis and Samuel Evans, *History of Lancaster County, Pennsylvania* (Philadelphia: Everts and Peck, 1883), pp. 508–509. Geist's three initials stand for Jacob Miller Willis. For his political role in the county, see the *Daily New Era*, 3 October 1879, p. 1.

17. *Daily New Era*, 10 September 1879, p. 2.

18. The case, involving illegal liquor sales, was heard in court in October, but was finally settled out of court when Geist and Warfel agreed to publish a retraction of the offending story. See the *Daily New Era*, 23, 24, and 25 October 1879, p. 4 in each instance.

19. "Martin, E[dwin] K." *Biographical Annals of Lancaster County, Pennsylvania* (1903).

20. E. K. Martin, *Oration* (Lancaster: The New Era Steam Book and Job Print, 1877), with prefacing note by J. M. W. Geist, p. 2.

21. *Daily New Era*, 23 October 1879, p. 4.

22. The district attorney, accused by Martin of shielding defendants in yet another illegal liquor sales case, in turn accused Martin, who was associated with him as assistant prosecutor, of agreeing to accept fifty dollars from the defendants to settle the case. The court cleared Martin of that charge, but fined him ten dollars for his indecorous language. See the *Daily New Era*, 19 and 26 August 1879, p. 4 in both instances. For Geist's editorial support of Martin, see the *Daily New Era*, 25 August 1879, p. 1.

23. *Progress*, 19 July 1879, pp. 704–706.

24. Mott, *American Journalism*, p. 450.

25. *Daily New Era*, 1 October 1879, p. 1.

CHAPTER 2

1. Walt Whitman, *Daybooks and Notebooks*, ed. William White (New York: New York University Press, 1978), II, *Daybooks, December 1881–1891*, p. 305, n.

2. War Department, Signal Service Corps, U.S. Army, Philadelphia Pennsylvania, table for September 1879.

3. The description is in his *The American Scene* (1907; rpt. Bloomington: Indiana University Press, 1968), p. 282.

4. Walt Whitman, *Prose Works 1892*, ed. Floyd Stovall (New York: New York University Press, 1963), I, *Specimen Days*, "The First Spring Day on Chestnut Street," pp. 188–190; from the *Philadelphia Progress*, 8 March 1879.

5. *Daybooks and Notebooks*, I, *Daybooks, 1876–November 1881*, p. 153.

6. Walt Whitman, *The Correspondence*, ed. Edwin Haviland Miller (New York: New York University Press, 1964), III, p. 117, n. 45; p. 158, n. 62.

7. Letter on *Progress* letterhead, 9 August 1879, John W. Forney to Judge J. S. Emery of the Invitations Committee, Old Settlers' Meeting; in

file of "Old Settlers' Quarter Centennial Celebration, 1879," Kansas State Historical Society, Topeka.

8. *Daybooks, 1876–November 1881*, p. 156, n. 735.

9. *Lancaster* (Pennsylvania) *Daily New Era*, 1 October 1879, p. 1. Evidently, Martin had gone to Philadelphia earlier, perhaps to confer with the *Philadelphia Press* editors about his correspondent's role.

10. *Specimen Days*, p. 205; contrast with *Daybooks, 1876–November 1881*, p. 156, n. 735.

11. For an account of the Pittsburgh riots, see Edwin P. Alexander, *The Pennsylvania Railroad, A Pictorial History* (New York: Bonanza Books, 1947), pp. 223–226. A company account is in George H. Burgess and Miles C. Kennedy, *Centennial History of the Pennsylvania Railroad Company* (Philadelphia: The Pennsylvania Railroad Company, 1949), pp. 365–373.

12. *Daybooks, 1876–November 1881*, p. 156, n. 735.

13. *Philadelphia Press*, 17 September 1879, p. 10.

14. Ibid.

15. Ibid.

16. *Specimen Days*, pp. 205–206. In his later poem "Orange Buds by Mail from Florida," first published in the *New York Herald*, 19 March 1888, Whitman returned to Voltaire's argument, suggesting that the delivery of orange buds in the North in less than three days was also proof of progress.

17. *The Correspondence*, III, letter #781, to Peter Doyle, 13 December 1876, p. 67.

18. *Specimen Days*, pp. 205–206.

19. *Urbana* (Ohio) *Citizen & Gazette*, 18 September 1879, p. 3; from a typescript furnished by the Champaign County Library, Urbana, Ohio.

20. *The Correspondence*, III, letter #934, to Louisa Whitman, 12–13 September 1879, pp. 163–164.

21. *Daily New Era*, 17 September 1879, p. 1.

22. From an album catalogued at the Princeton University Library as Philip Ashton Rollins, "Walt Whitman, Autograph notes made during his railway journey from Camden, N. J. to Colorado and return, September 10, 1879 to January 5, 1880," p. 2; also edited and published as "Walt Whitman's Notes on His Western Trip," *Biblia* 1 (June 1930): [3].

23. *The Correspondence*, III, letter #934, to Louisa Whitman, 12–13 September 1879, p. 164.

24. *Specimen Days*, p. 205. See also p. 206; within a dozen lines (in two succeeding sections) Whitman employs the trite lightning simile.

25. *Daily New Era*, 17 September 1879, p. 1. Geist apparently didn't

share Whitman's later expressed enthusiasm for the prairies. His attitude is closer to that of Charles Dickens, who visited Illinois in 1842 and found the prairie there "oppressive in its barren monotony." See his *American Notes and Pictures from Italy* (London: Chapman & Hall, n.d.), pp. 216–217.

26. *The Correspondence*, III, letter #934, to Louisa Whitman, 12–13 September 1879, p. 164. Whitman indicates here that the party arrived in St. Louis around 10:30 A.M.; Forney, however, reported in *Progress*, 20 September 1879, p. 881, that they arrived at 5 A.M. Geist's comment about awaking sixty-eight miles from St. Louis suggests a fairly early arrival. The train was reported as three hours late in the *Missouri Republican*, 13 September 1879, p. 3.

27. *Daily New Era*, 17 September 1879, p. 1; Dickens, *American Notes and Pictures from Italy*, p. 207. Dickens stayed at the Planters' when it was a new hotel. He was among the earliest of a number of illustrious guests, including Lincoln and Grant, who stopped there. For a history of the hotel, see Dorothy Garasche Holland, "The Planters' House," *Missouri Historical Society Bulletin* 28 (January, 1972): 109–117.

28. *The Correspondence*, III, letter # 934, to Louisa Whitman, 12–13 September 1879, p. 164.

29. *Missouri Republican*, 13 September 1879, p. 3.

30. *Daily New Era*, 17 September 1879, p. 1.

31. *Press*, 17 September 1879, p. 10.

32. *St. Louis Daily Globe-Democrat*, 13 September 1879, p. 6.

33. *Missouri Republican*, 13 September 1879, p. 3. This description was repeated the next day in the *Kansas City* (Missouri) *Daily Times*, 14 September 1879, p. 2.

34. *St. Louis Daily Globe-Democrat*, 13 September 1879, p. 6.

35. Ibid. Whitman's conditions about no public dinners and speeches were announced the same day in the *Philadelphia Inquirer*, p. 4.

36. *Missouri Republican*, 13 September 1879, p. 3.

37. Ibid.; also *St. Louis Daily Globe-Democrat*, 13 September 1879, p. 6.

38. *St. Louis Daily Globe-Democrat*, 13 September 1879, p. 6.

39. Ibid. These statements were given wide circulation by Whitman's companions; in the *Daily New Era*, 17 September 1879, p. 2; and in the *Press*, 17 September 1879, p. 4. They were also quoted in a brief notice in the *Atchison* (Kansas) *Globe*, 30 September 1879, p. 1.

40. *St. Louis Daily Globe-Democrat*, 13 September 1879, p. 6.

41. *Daily New Era*, 19 September 1879, p. 1.

42. *Daybooks, 1876–November 1881*, p. 164, n. 741a.

43. *Specimen Days,* pp. 206–207.

44. J. Johnston, M. D. and J. W. Wallace, *Visits to Walt Whitman in 1890–1891* (New York: Washington Square Bookshop, 1918), p. 140.

45. *Daily New Era,* 19 September 1879, p. 1.

46. Ibid., 17 September 1879, p. 1. Kersey Coates (1823–1887), Free Soiler and Civil War officer, was an early Kansas City builder and promoter. His Coates Opera House (1870–1901) was a famous theatrical landmark. His Coates House (1005 Broadway) was a leading hotel in the city from about 1869 to well into the twentieth century. Now on the National Register of Historic Places it still stands, though severely damaged by fire on 28 January 1978.

47. *Daily New Era,* 19 September 1879, p. 1; *Specimen Days,* p. 207. Besides Crawford, the awaiting committee included, according to Geist, Judge J. S. Emery, Sidney Clarke, John Hutchings, John Speer, and a Dr. Swander.

48. *Press,* 20 September 1879, p. 8.

CHAPTER 3

1. *Lawrence* (Kansas) *Daily Journal,* 11 September 1879, p. 4.

2. *Lancaster* (Pennsylvania) *Daily New Era,* 19 September 1879, p. 1. The Ludington was on the site of today's Eldridge House. John and Margaret Usher had four sons: Arthur (b. 1846), John, Jr. (b. 1849), Linton (b. 1852), and Samuel (b. 1855). Apparently only John, Jr., and Linton were at home at the time of Whitman's visit.

3. Robert R. Hubach, "Walt Whitman and the West" (Ph.D. diss., Indiana University, 1943), p. 169. The Usher house, at 1425 Tennessee Street, became a fraternity house in 1912, and with an added rear dormitory wing still serves that purpose.

4. Elmo R. Richardson and Alan W. Farley, *John Palmer Usher: Lincoln's Secretary of Interior* (Lawrence, Kansas: University of Kansas Press, 1960), pp. 29–32; 79–84; 86–108; 134, n. 36. It is curious that, writing in *November Boughs* (1888) about Lincoln's interior secretaries, Whitman forgot Usher's succession after Caleb Smith. See *Prose Works 1892,* ed. Floyd Stovall (New York: New York University Press, 1964), II, *Collect and Other Prose,* pp. 611–612. The scroll presented to Usher, cited by Richardson and Farley as in the Usher Papers at the Kansas State Historical Society, Topeka, is now lost.

5. *Daily New Era,* 19 September 1879, p. 1.

6. Richardson and Farley, *Usher,* p. 110. Among other features, the

house had dark walnut panelling trimmed in gold leaf (done by Pullman Palace Car Company craftsmen), a monogrammed staircase, and a dark marble fireplace (a gift from Usher's fellow cabinet members).

7. Documents relative to Whitman's dismissal are in Horace Traubel, *With Walt Whitman in Camden* (New York: Mitchell Kennerly, 1914), III, *November 1, 1888–January 20, 1889*, pp. 470–471; and in Dixon Wecter, "Walt Whitman as Civil Servant," *PMLA* 58 (December 1943); 1094–1109. A good account of the episode is in Jerome Loving, *Walt Whitman's Champion: William Douglas O'Connor* (College Station: Texas A & M University Press, 1978), pp. 54–59.

8. Hubach, "Walt Whitman and the West," p. 168.

9. Walt Whitman, *Prose Works 1892*, ed. Floyd Stovall (New York: New York University Press, 1963), I, *Specimen Days*, p. 208.

10. For these and other details of the Lawrence scene, see the *Lawrence Daily Journal*, 16 September 1879, pp. 1, 4; and the (Lawrence) *Kansas Daily Tribune*, 15 September 1879, p. 4.

11. *Daily Journal*, 16 September 1879, p. 4.

12. *Kansas Daily Tribune*, 15 September 1879, p. 4.

13. *Daily Journal*, 4 September 1879, p. 1; 10 September 1879, p. 4; 13 September 1879, p. 4.

14. See Jim L. Lewis, " 'Beautiful Bismarck'—Bismarck Grove, Lawrence, 1878–1900," *Kansas Historical Quarterly* 35 (Autumn 1969): 225–256. The grove no longer exists; in its place is an alfalfa field.

15. *Daily New Era*, 19 September, 1879, p. 1.

16. War Department, Signal Service Corps, U.S. Army, Lawrence, Kansas, table for September 1879.

17. *Kansas Daily Tribune*, 16 September 1879, pp. 1, 4; *Daily Journal*, 17 September 1879, p. 4.

18. *Progress*, 4 October 1879, p. 923; *Daily New Era*, 3 October 1879, p. 1.

19. *Progress*, 4 October 1879, pp. 924, 925. There were in fact many ex-Pennsylvanians at the grove. Of the approximately 3500 early settlers who signed the official register, 277 gave Pennsylvania as their birthplace. Fourteen of those were from Lancaster County, including Isaac Sharp, attorney of Council Grove, who had once been a Kansas gubernatorial candidate (1870), and who apparently gave Whitman his card. The original register is at the Kansas State Historical Society, Topeka; a roughly alphabetized version of it is in Charles A. Gleed, ed., *The Kansas Memorial, A Report of the Old Settlers' Meeting Held at Bismarck Grove, Kansas, September 15 and 16th, 1879* (Kansas City, Missouri: Ramsey, Millett and Hudson, 1880),

pp. 211–255. For Sharp's card, see Walt Whitman, *Daybooks and Note-books*, ed. William White (New York: New York University Press, 1978), I, *Daybooks, 1876–November, 1881*, p. 159.

20. *Daily Journal*, 16 September 1879, p. 1.

21. Ibid., 17 September 1879, p. 4.

22. Gleed, ed., *Kansas Memorial*, pp. 15–16. Work (1832–1884), an abolitionist, is better known for his "Marching through Georgia," "Grandfather's Clock," and, especially, "Come Home, Father" ("Father, dear, Father, come home with me now!"). It is curious that his song is identified in the *Memorial* as written by Whitman, and so reported in at least one paper, the *Topeka* (Kansas) *Commonwealth*, 16 September 1879, p. 3.

23. Gleed, ed., *Kansas Memorial*, pp. 49, 78, 160.

24. Ibid., p. 96. The letter, dated 29 August 1879, is at the Kansas State Historical Society, Topeka. A full account of Whittier's Kansas connection is in Cora Colbee, *Kansas and "The Prairied West" of John G. Whittier* (Essex Institute Historical Collections, 1945; rpt. n.p., 1946).

25. *Daily Journal*, 17 September 1879, p. 2.

26. Gleed, ed., *Kansas Memorial*, pp. 11–15, 17–23, 30–32, 25–29, 48–87.

27. Ibid., pp. 35–48.

28. Ibid., pp. 140–148. Hale's book *Kanzas and Nebraska* (1854), which, in its descriptions of the territory, had been a useful guide to emigrants, may have been as well known among some of the Old Settlers as his later story "The Man Without a Country" (1863).

29. Hale's review is in the *North American Review* 82 (January 1856); 275–277.

30. *Daily Journal*, 16 September 1879, p. 1.

31. *Progress*, 4 October 1879, p. 923.

32. An account of Whitman's position against the extension of slavery within the context of his nationalism is in Walt Whitman, *The Eighteenth Presidency!* ed. Edward F. Grier (Lawrence, Kansas: University of Kansas Press, 1956), pp. 1–18. For an account of Whitman's editorship of the *Free-man*, see Joseph Jay Rubin, *The Historic Whitman* (University Park: Pennsylvania University Press, 1973), pp. 210–222.

33. *Kansas Magazine* 1 (February 1872): 113–114; 1 (March 1872): 219.

34. Walt Whitman, *Prose Works 1892*, ed. Floyd Stovall (New York: New York University Press, 1964), II, *Collect and Other Prose*, p. 384.

35. *St. Louis Daily Globe-Democrat*, 13 September 1879, p. 6.

36. The Old Settlers apparently misunderstood Whitman's visit from the outset. As early as August 31 it was announced that he would "deliver a

poem." See the *Lawrence Daily Journal*, 31 August 1879, p. 2. For Tuesday, September 16, a program published in the same paper listed for 3:30 P.M. an address by the Honorable T. D. Thacher "introductory to poem by Walt Whitman." *Daily Journal*, 14 September 1879, p. 4. On the seventeenth a Kansas City paper indicated that the committee on arrangements erred in expecting a poem by Whitman, because he was attending the meeting "by invitation of Col. Forney merely as a traveling companion." See *Kansas City* (Missouri) *Daily Journal*, 17 September 1879, p. 5.

37. Gleed, ed., *Kansas Memorial*, p. 153.
38. *Lawrence Daily Journal*, 16 September 1879, p. 1.
39. Hubach, "Walt Whitman and the West," pp. 168, 172.
40. William Monroe Balch, "The Education of Linton Usher," *Indiana Magazine of History* 34 (December 1938): 402–408.
41. Hubach, "Walt Whitman and the West," p. 172.
42. *Specimen Days*, p. 207. Whitman erroneously locates the Silver Wedding meeting at Topeka.
43. Ibid., p. 208.
44. Hubach, "Walt Whitman and the West," p. 174.

CHAPTER 4

1. *Topeka* (Kansas) *Commonwealth*, 17 September 1879, p. 2; *Lancaster* (Pennsylvania) *Daily New Era*, 1 October 1879, p. 1.
2. *Topeka Daily Blade*, 18 September 1879, p. 4.
3. The figure is from the 1880 census; taken from Chas. S. Gleed, ed., *From River to Sea; A Tourists' and Miners' Guide . . .* (Chicago: Rand, McNally & Co., 1882), p. 15.
4. Walt Whitman, *Prose Works 1892*, ed. Floyd Stovall (New York: New York University Press, 1963), I, *Specimen Days*, p. 207.
5. *Progress*, 4 October 1879, p. 924.
6. *Daily New Era*, 8 October 1879, p. 1; *Progress*, 4 October 1879, pp. 924–925.
7. *Daily New Era*, 3 October 1879, p. 1.
8. See, for example, *Progress*, 4 October 1879, p. 924; *Philadelphia Press*, 19 September 1879, p. 5; 24 September 1879, pp. 4, 8; *Daily New Era*, 25 September 1879, p. 1.
9. In an album catalogued at the Princeton University Library as Philip Ashton Rollins, "Walt Whitman, Autograph notes made during his railway journey from Camden, N. J. to Colorado and return, September 10, 1879, to January 5, 1880," p. 1. This note, evidently thought indecipherable, was not

published with the other notes of the album in "Walt Whitman's Notes of His Western Trip," *Biblia* 1 (June 1930).

10. *Daily New Era*, 8 October 1879, p. 1.

11. *Commonwealth*, 18 September 1879, p. 3.

12. *Daily New Era*, 8 October 1879, p. 1.

13. *Specimen Days*, p. 207.

14. Rollins, "Walt Whitman's Autograph notes . . . ," album, p. 9; published in *Biblia* 1 (June 1930) : [3].

15. *Commonwealth*, 18 September 1879, p. 3.

16. Ibid., 17 September 1879, p. 3.

17. Ibid., 18 September 1879, p. 3.

18. Ibid., 16 September 1879, p. 3.

19. *Topeka Daily Blade*, 16 September 1879, p. 4. Forney's lecture, advertised also as "What I Know About Our Public Men," was apparently drawn from his *Anecdotes of Public Men*, the first volume of which had appeared in 1873. He was to bring out a second volume in 1881.

20. *Commonwealth*, 18 September 1879, p. 3; *Topeka Daily Capital*, 18 September 1879, p. 4.

21. *Daily Capital*, 18 September 1879, p. 4.

22. *Commonwealth*, 19 September 1879, p. 3.

23. Rollins, "Walt Whitman, Autograph notes . . . ," album, p. 9; published in *Biblia* 1 (June 1930) : [3].

24. Sidney H. Morse, "My Summer With Walt Whitman, 1887," in *In Re Walt Whitman*, ed. Horace Traubel, Richard Maurice Bucke, and Thomas B. Harned (Philadelphia: David McKay, 1893), pp. 382–383.

25. *Commonwealth*, 19 September 1879, p. 3.

26. *Daily New Era*, 1 October 1879, p. 1; *Daily Blade*, 18 September 1879, p. 4.

27. *Daily New Era*, 19 September 1879, p. 1.

28. Ibid., 8 October 1879, p. 1.

29. Ibid., 10 October 1879, p. 1. The party's leisurely dining, as at Lexington Junction days earlier, is in sharp contrast to what Robert Louis Stevenson describes of the haste of taking meals on an emigrant train on the Union Pacific Railroad the same year. See his *From Scotland to Silverado*, ed. James D. Hart (Cambridge, Massachusetts: The Belknap Press of Harvard University Press, 1966), pp. 119–121.

30. *Daily New Era*, 10 October 1879, p. 1. The frontier incident is in *Specimen Days*, p. 209.

31. Walt Whitman, *The Correspondence*, ed. Edwin Haviland Miller

(New York: New York University Press, 1964), III, letter #935, to Louisa Orr Whitman, 19 September 1879, p. 165.

32. Charles S. Gleed, ed., *The Kansas Memorial, A Report of the Old Settlers' Meeting Held at Bismarck Grove, Kansas, September 15 and 16, 1879* (Kansas City, Missouri: Ramsey, Millett and Hudson, 1880), p. [4]. The lines are from "Europe, the 72nd and 73d Years of These States," first published as "Resurgemus," *New York Daily Tribune*, June 21, 1850, and subsequently as one of the twelve untitled poems of *Leaves of Grass*, 1855.

33. Rollins, "Walt Whitman, Autograph notes . . . ," album, pp. 3, 5, 7; published in *Biblia* 1 (June 1930): [3]. See Whitman's use of these memoranda in *Specimen Days*, p. 219.

34. *Daily New Era*, 15 October 1879, p. 1.

35. Ibid.

36. Whitman, *The Correspondence*, III, letter #935, to Louisa Orr Whitman, 19 September 1879, p. 165.

CHAPTER 5

1. Robert L. Perkin, *The First Hundred Years, An Informal History of Denver and the Rocky Mountain News* (Garden City, New York: Doubleday and Company, 1959), pp. 347–350.

2. *Denver Post*, 1 August 1926, p. 3; 17 December 1933, p. 13. The building was demolished in 1933.

3. Don L. Griswold and Jean Harvey Griswold, *The Carbonate Camp Called Leadville* (Denver: University of Denver Press, 1951), p. 98.

4. From Kansas Pacific Railway advertisements: *Lawrence* (Kansas) *Daily Journal*, 14 September 1879, p. 3; (Lawrence) *Kansas Daily Tribune*, 15 September 1879, p. 3; *Topeka* (Kansas) *Daily Blade*, 16 September 1879, p. 3.

5. Griswold, *The Carbonate Camp Called Leadville*, pp. 98–99.

6. Clara Barrus, *Whitman and Burroughs—Comrades* (1931; rpt. Port Washington, New York: Kennikat Press, 1968), opp. p. 188; Herbert H. Gilchrist, ed., *Anne Gilchrist, Her Life and Writings* (London: T. Fisher Unwin. 1887), opp. p. 253. Whitman's notebook indicates that he sent similar maps to his sisters, Hannah Heyde and Mary Van Nostrand; to Louisa Orr Whitman; and to Crosby S. Noyes, editor of the *Washington* (D.C.) *Evening Star*. See Walt Whitman, *Daybooks and Notebooks*, ed. William White (New York: New York University Press, 1978), I, *Daybooks, 1876–November 1881*, p. 161.

7. *Washington* (D.C.) *Evening Star*, 30 September 1879, p. 1. The same

item appeared in the *Philadelphia Weekly Times*, 4 October 1879, p. 7.

8. Walt Whitman, *Prose Works 1892*, ed. Floyd Stovall (New York: New York University Press, 1963), I, *Specimen Days*, pp. 209, 210.

9. See advertisement, Wall and Witters' coach line, *Denver Daily News*, 20 September 1879, p. 8. "Garos" (sometimes "Garo") derives phonetically from the French "Guiraud" ("Guyraud" in Geist's spelling), the name of two brothers, Henry and Adolph, who settled in the area around 1863. See M. C. Poor, *Denver, South Park and Pacific* (Denver: Rocky Mountain Railroad Club, 1976), Memorial Edition, p. 424.

10. On 23 July 1880, the Denver and Rio Grande Railway reached Leadville via the Arkansas River canyon. That fall the Denver, South Park and Pacific began sharing the Rio Grande trackage. The South Park's alternate "High Line" reached Leadville from the northeast on 1 February 1884. See Griswold, *The Carbonate Camp Called Leadville*, pp. 134, 150, n. 40.

11. Griswold, *The Carbonate Camp Called Leadville*, pp. 100–109.

12. Walt Whitman, *The Correspondence*, ed. Edwin Haviland Miller (New York: New York University Press, 1964), III, letter #935 to Louisa Orr Whitman, 19 September 1879, p. 165.

13. *Philadelphia Press*, 2 October 1879, p. 5.

14. *Lancaster* (Pennsylvania) *Daily New Era*, 1 October 1879, p. 1. These plans must have been made the Friday afternoon or evening before (if not by correspondence earlier), for they were announced in a "Distinguished Arrivals" item in the *Denver Daily Republican* on Saturday morning, 20 September 1879, p. 1. Tough's middle initial is "S," not "T" as Geist gives it. As the plans worked out, the reunion on Monday was at Red Hill.

15. *Specimen Days*, p. 215.

16. Ibid., pp. 215–216. See also Rollo G. Silver, "Whitman Interviews Himself," *American Literature* 10 (March 1938): 84–87.

17. *Camden Daily Post*, 26 September 1879, p. 2. The entire article is in *Specimen Days*, Appendix, pp. 343–345. The inclusion of his plan to go "to the mountains by the South Park road to-morrow" is further evidence that the item appeared in the *Denver Tribune* of Sunday, 21 September 1879.

18. *Specimen Days*, pp. 210–211.

19. Ibid., pp. 211–212.

20. Ibid., pp. 212–213.

21. *Philadelphia Press*, 2 October 1879, p. 5. Eicholtz's diary, at the American Heritage Center, University of Wyoming, Laramie, confirms that he went "to end of track at Guirauds" that Saturday, 20 September 1879.

22. It is a coincidence that Geist, who was headed for court on a libel

charge, and Martin, who had just been fined on a contempt-of-court charge, are here being driven by a man who the year before had been acquitted of a murder charge. See *Topeka Commonwealth,* 18 December 1879, p. 2, for the account of a Jackson County, Kansas, railroad strike in which the strikers were fired upon by a sheriff's posse including Tough, then a U. S. marshal. A dozen shots were fired, including one, allegedly from Tough's gun, that killed one man. The jury found Tough not guilty after only eighteen minutes' deliberation; there was no evidence that he had fired the fatal shot. It is another coincidence that Tough, after a career in Colorado, later in the 1880s raced horses at Bismarck Grove, and still later, in 1900, bought the grove and turned it into a supply station for a horse and mule business in Kansas City. See Jim L. Lewis, " 'Beautiful Bismarck'—Bismarck Grove, Lawrence, 1878–1900," *Kansas Historical Quarterly* 35 (Autumn, 1969) : 256.

23. *Philadelphia Press,* 2 October 1879, p. 5.

24. *Daily New Era,* 1 October 1879, p. 1. Earlier Geist had described the staging as a 35-mile ride, which agrees with Martin's description of a 140-mile "plunge" into the Rockies, 105 of the miles by train. Geist is likening their ride to the one Hank Monk (not Smith) was supposed to have given Horace Greeley from Folsom to Placerville in California in 1859. The story as told by Charles Farrar Browne (Artemus Ward) is given in full in Don C. Seitz, *Horace Greeley* (Indianapolis: Bobbs-Merrill, 1926), pp. 302–306. See Mark Twain's handling of the episode in *Roughing It,* Chapter 20.

25. *Daily New Era,* 1 October 1879, p. 1.

26. Ibid.

27. *Philadelphia Press,* 2 October 1879, p. 5.

28. *Daily New Era,* 1 October 1879, p. 1. Geist is here likening their ride to the one in William Cowper's poem, "The Diverting History of John Gilpin."

29. *Daily New Era,* 1 October 1879, p. 1.

30. Ibid. Also *Denver Daily Republican,* 23 September 1879, p. 1.

CHAPTER 6

1. Walt Whitman, *Prose Works 1892,* ed. Floyd Stovall (New York: New York University Press, 1963), I, *Specimen Days,* p. 214.

2. *Denver* (Colorado) *Daily Republican,* 23 September 1879, p. 1; *Lancaster* (Pennsylvania) *Daily New Era,* 1 October 1879, p. 1; *Specimen Days,* p. 216.

3. *Specimen Days,* p. 217.

4. Walt Whitman, *The Correspondence,* ed. Edwin Haviland Miller

(New York: New York University Press, 1964), III, letter #939, to Peter Doyle, 5 November 1879, p. 168.

5. *Daily New Era*, 1 October 1879, p. 1.

6. In an album catalogued at the Princeton University Library as Philip Ashton Rollins, "Walt Whitman, Autograph notes made during his railway journey from Camden, N. J., to Colorado and return, September 10, 1879 to January 5, 1880," p. 19; published in *Biblia* 1 (June 1930): [3].

7. *Specimen Days*, p. 217.

8. Ibid., pp. 217–218.

9. Ibid., p. 220.

10. Walt Whitman, *Daybooks and Notebooks*, ed. William White (New York: New York University Press, 1978), I, *Daybooks, 1876–November 1881*, p. 156, n. 735.

11. Rollins, "Walt Whitman, Autograph notes . . . ," album, p. 3; published in *Biblia* 1 (June 1930): [3].

12. *Specimen Days*, p. 218; "coreopsis" also appears in a list of "perennial blossoms and friendly weeds I have made acquaintance with hereabout one season or another in my walks," p. 180.

13. *Daily New Era*, 1 October 1879, p. 1; *Specimen Days*, p. 218.

14. *Correspondence*, III, letter #939, to Peter Doyle, 5 November 1879, p. 168. Whitman says Lindsey was "running *the* hotel [emphasis added]" in Sterling. There were at least three hotels there in 1879, according to newspaper advertisements: the Broadway Hotel, the Green Mountain House, and the Cottage Hotel. It is curious that the business card which Lindsey gave to Whitman does not indicate the hotel. See *Daybooks, 1876–November 1881*, p. 158.

15. *Daily New Era*, 8 October 1879, p. 1.

16. Ibid., 1 October 1879, p. 1.

17. *Sterling* (Kansas) *Weekly Bulletin*, 25 September 1879, p. 3.

18. (Sterling, Kansas) *Rice County Gazette*, 25 September 1879, p. 7.

19. Ibid.

20. *Correspondence*, III, letter #939, p. 168.

21. *Specimen Days*, pp. 218–219.

22. *Daily New Era*, 1 October 1879, p. 1.

23. *Kansas City* (Missouri) *Daily Times*, 26 September 1879, p. 3.

24. *Specimen Days*, p. 228.

25. *Daily New Era*, 1 October 1879, p. 1.

26. *Daily Times*, 27 September 1879, p. 4. The tone of this item is explainable in part by the fact that the *Times*, in editorial debate that same

day (p. 2) with the *Kansas City Mail* (see that paper, p. 4) was protesting what it saw as dishonest timing and general lawlessness at the racetrack. In particular, it objected to having Kersey Coates officiate at races in which his hotel guests were running horses.

27. *Specimen Days*, pp. 225–226.

28. *Daily Times*, 28 September 1879, p. 4. This same item entire was quoted in the *Lawrence* (Kansas) *Daily Journal*, 1 October 1879, p. 2.

29. *Daily Times*, 27 September 1879, p. 3.

30. *Daily New Era*, 1 October 1879, p. 1.

CHAPTER 7

1. *St. Louis Daily Globe-Democrat*, 13 September 1879, p. 6.

2. *Lancaster* (Pennsylvania) *Daily New Era*, 30 September 1879, p. 4.

3. Walt Whitman, *The Correspondence*, ed. Edwin Haviland Miller (New York: New York University Press, 1964), III, letter #936, to Louisa Orr Whitman, 11 October 1879, p. 166. See also *The Correspondence*, VI, *A Supplement with a Composite Index* (1977), letter #936.5, to Richard Maurice Bucke, 17 October 1879, p. 21, in which Whitman writes "shall stay here twelve days."

4. See *The Correspondence*, III, letter #938, to Robert Underwood Johnson, 29 October 1879, p. 167; #939, to Peter Doyle, 5 November 1879, p. 168; and #941, to John Burroughs, 23 November 1879, p. 171.

5. *The Correspondence*, III, letter #939, to Peter Doyle, 5 November 1879, p. 168.

6. Ibid., letter #940, to Anne Gilchrist, 10 November 1879, p. 169.

7. Ibid., letter #936, to Louisa Orr Whitman, 11 October 1879, p. 165.

8. Ibid., p. 166.

9. Walt Whitman, *Prose Works 1892*, ed. Floyd Stovall (New York: New York University Press, 1963), I, *Specimen Days*, p. 228, n. 22.

10. *Specimen Days*, p. 228.

11. *The Correspondence*, III, letter #936, to Louisa Orr Whitman, 11 October 1879, p. 166.

12. Ibid., letter #941, to John Burroughs, 23 November 1879, p. 170; Walt Whitman, *Daybooks and Notebooks*, ed. William White (New York: New York University Press, 1978), I, *Daybooks, 1876–November 1881*, p. 165, n. 741a. Whitman errs in locating the library on Fourth Street.

13. *The Correspondence*, III, letter #941, to John Burroughs, 23 November 1879, p. 171. Both Harris and Brokmeyer gave Whitman their cards: see *Daybooks, 1876–November 1881*, pp. 158, 160. In his letter to Burroughs

Whitman noted that Amos Bronson Alcott was expected in St. Louis, but if Whitman saw him there he made no note of their meeting.

14. *The Correspondence*, III, letter #937, to William Torrey Harris, 27 October 1879, pp. 166–167.

15. The public kindergarten in America originated in part in St. Louis where Susan Blow (1843–1916) held her first class in 1873. By the time of Whitman's stay there, kindergartens, with Harris's support, were well established in the St. Louis school system, though they were still experimental in many other parts of the United States. See Elizabeth Dale Ross, *The Kindergarten Crusade: The Establishment of Preschool Education in the United States* (Athens, Ohio): Ohio University Press, 1976), pp. 12–16.

16. Horace Traubel, *With Walt Whitman in Camden* (New York: Mitchell Kennerley, 1914), III, *November 1, 1888–January 20, 1889*, p. 412.

17. *Daily New Era*, 17 September 1879, p. 1.

18. *The Correspondence*, III, letter #939, to Peter Doyle, 5 November 1879, p. 169.

19. Ibid., letter #943, to John Burroughs, 2 [3] January 1879, p. 172.

20. *Specimen Days*, p. 229.

21. *Daybooks, 1876–November 1881*, p. 160.

22. Ibid., pp. 159–160.

23. Walt Whitman, *Prose Works 1892*, ed. Floyd Stovall (New York: New York University Press, 1964), II, *Collect and Other Prose*, pp. 582–583.

24. *St. Louis Daily Globe-Democrat*, 7 November 1879, p. 2.

25. *Collect and Other Prose*, p. 583.

26. *Globe-Democrat*, 7 November 1879, p. 2.

27. *Collect and Other Prose*, pp. 583–584.

28. *Daybooks, 1876–November 1881*, pp. 158–162.

29. *Specimen Days*, pp. 226–227.

30. *New York Times*, 21 September 1879, p. 1.

31. Ibid., 16 September 1879, p. 1.

32. *Lawrence* (Kansas) *Daily Journal*, 2 September 1879, p. 4; 27 September 1879, p. 1.

33. *New York Times*, 29 September 1879, p. 1; 1 October 1879, p. 5.

34. *Specimen Days*, pp. 226–227, n.

35. Ibid., p. 227, n.

36. Ibid., pp. 222–227.

37. *The Correspondence*, III, letter #936, to Louisa Orr Whitman, 11 October 1879, p. 166.

38. *Daybooks, 1876–November 1881*, p. 161; see also *The Correspondence*, III, p. 170, n. 7.

39. *Camden Daily Post*, 20 December 1879, p. 2, following Grant's triumphal return to Philadelphia on December 15, 1879; a few typographical errors have been corrected, and a different series of symbols substituted for references.

40. *Specimen Days*, pp. 224–225.

41. *St. Louis Post-Dispatch*, 17 October 1879, p. 2; a few typographical matters edited. I note that this piece (with one sentence of the next-to-last paragraph inadvertently omitted) was first published for scholars in Robert R. Hubach, "Three Uncollected St. Louis Interviews of Walt Whitman," *American Literature* 14 (May 1942): 141–147.

42. *The Correspondence*, III, letter #938, to Robert Underwood Johnson, 29 October 1879, p. 167; Robert Underwood Johnson, *Remembered Yestedays* (Boston: Little, Brown and Company, 1923), p. 335.

43. Johnson, *Remembered Yesterdays*, pp. 335–337. This "interview" Whitman did apparently forward to several friendly editors in the East, for it was quoted in part by Geist in the *Daily New Era*, 21 October 1879, p. 2; partially published in two issues of the *Camden Daily Post*, 23 October 1879, p. 1, and 25 October 1879, p. 2; and published in part in the *Philadelphia Weekly Times*, 25 October 1879, p. 7.

44. *St. Louis Daily Globe-Democrat*, 22 November 1879, p. 6; *Washington Evening Star*, 15 November 1879, p. 1. The two items are virtually identical.

45. *Daily New Era*, 30 September 1879, p. 4.

46. Ibid., 25 November 1879, p. 2.

47. *Camden Daily Post*, 1 December 1879, p. 1.

CHAPTER 8

1. Walt Whitman, *The Correspondence*, ed. Edwin Haviland Miller (New York: New York University Press, 1964), III, letter #941, to John Burroughs, 23 November 1879, p. 171.

2. Ibid., letter #943, to John Burroughs, 2 January 1890, p. 172 with n. 1.

3. Letter on *Progress* letterhead, 9 August 1879, John W. Forney to Judge J. S. Emery of the Invitations Committee, Old Settlers' Meeting; in file of "Old Settlers' Quarter Centennial Celebration, 1879," Kansas State Historical Society, Topeka.

4. Walt Whitman, *Daybooks and Notebooks*, ed. William White (New

York: New York University Press, 1978), I, *Daybooks, 1876–November 1881*, p. 165.

5. In album catalogued at the Princeton University Library as Philip Ashton Rollins, "Walt Whitman, Autograph notes made during his railway journey from Camden, N. J. to Colorado and return, September 10, 1879 to January 5, 1880," p. 13; edited and published as "Walt Whitman's Notes of His Western Trip," *Biblia* 1 (June 1930): [3].

6. Rollins, "Walt Whitman, Autograph notes . . . ," album, p. 15; published in *Biblia* 1 (June 1930): [3].

7. *Daybooks, 1876–November 1881*, p. 165.

8. *Camden Daily Post*, 7 January 1880, p. 1. The reference to Whitman's return "yesterday" suggests that he had intended the item for Tuesday's paper. "August" must be simply a slip of memory. It is worth recording that when this news story was quoted in Bucke's biography of Whitman, these lines from the second paragraph were omitted: ". . . and considers the trip the most valuable revelation of his life. He has not yet written out his impressions and notes, but will soon do so." See R. M. Bucke, *Walt Whitman* (Philadelphia: David McKay, 1883), p. 221. We know now that Whitman himself made the deletions. See *Walt Whitman's Autograph Revision of the Analysis of Leaves of Grass* (New York: New York University Press, 1974), p. 168.

9. *The Correspondence*, VI, *A Supplement with a Composite Index* (1977), pp. xix-xxi.

10. Gay Wilson Allen, *The Solitary Singer* (New York: The Macmillan Co., 1955), p. 488.

11. *Washington Evening Star*, 27 March 1880, p. 6, reporting "Camden letter in Philadelphia *Times*."

12. Walt Whitman, *Prose Works 1892*, ed. Floyd Stovall (New York: New York University Press, 1963), I, *Specimen Days*, pp. 229–230.

13. Rollins, "Walt Whitman, Autograph notes . . . ," album, p. 17; published in *Biblia* 1 (June 1930): [3].

14. *Specimen Days*, p. 1.

15. Ibid. Whitman's date for this entry, July 2, 1882, is not supported by his daybook, which has no entry for July 2 but does note "three days at Glendale, 3d, 4th, 5th July." See Walt Whitman, *Daybooks and Notebooks*, ed. William White (New York: New York University Press, 1978), II, *Daybooks, December 1881–1891*, p. 297. Glendale, Kirkwood, White Horse, Timber Creek (and, today, Laurel Springs) are all names associated with the Stafford Farm.

16. *The Correspondence*, III, letter #1133, to Rees Welsh and Company, 20 June 1882, p. 292.

17. Ibid., letter #1099, to James R. Osgood & Company, 21 March 1882, p. 269.

18. *Daybooks, December 1881–1891*, p. 297. For another discussion of the composing of *Specimen Days*, see Linck C. Johnson, "The Design of Walt Whitman's *Specimen Days*," *Walt Whitman Review* 21 (March 1975): 3–14. I am in accord here with some of the initial points of that essay. See also Alfred Kazin's Introduction to *Specimen Days* (Boston: David R. Godine, 1971), pp. xix–xxiv.

19. *Specimen Days*, pp. 206, 207, 226.

20. The Civil War sections of *Specimen Days* are, of course, another story.

21. Allen, *The Solitary Singer*, p. 510.

22. *Specimen Days*, p. 293.

Bibliographical Essay

As the notes indicate, I have relied in this work on a wide range of materials, and have incurred many debts of scholarship which I know fair and accurate citations can only partially repay. Of all that documentation I would here single out those sources upon which I have a special dependence, and which help characterize this book.

Central to my study are several volumes of the *Collected Writings of Walt Whitman*, General Editors Gay Wilson Allen and Sculley Bradley, published by the New York University Press. I use as basic texts: *Prose Works 1892*, ed. Floyd Stovall, I, *Specimen Days*, 1963; II, *Collect and Other Prose*, 1964; *The Correspondence*, ed. Edwin Haviland Miller, III, 1964; and VI, *A Supplement with a Composite Index*, 1977. The last, in its Introduction, has much valuable information about the business side of Whitman's career. Also necessary to the life of the study are the *Daybooks and Notebooks*, ed. William White, I, *Daybooks, 1876–November 1881*, 1978; II, *Daybooks, December 1881–1891*, 1978; and III, *Diary in Canada, Notebooks, Index*, 1978. The first volume is especially important to my purpose, incorporating as it does (with some corrections) Rena V. Grant, "The Livezey-Whitman Manuscripts," *Walt Whitman Review* 7 (March 1961): 3–14, containing a transcription of Whitman's notebook for the trip (now at the University of California at Berkeley).

Supplementing the *Daybooks and Notebooks* are autograph notes on the trip in the Western Americana Collections at Princeton University. These consist of eleven (originally ten) sets of notes in pencil and ink. Mounted in an album catalogued at the Princeton University Library as Philip Ashton Rollins, "Walt Whitman, Autograph notes made during his railway journey from Camden, N.J. to Colorado and return, September 10, 1879 to January 5, 1880." Once owned by Carolyn Wells (see *Whitman at Auction, 1899–1972*, compiled by Gloria A. Francis and Artem Lozynsky, 1978, pp. 58–60, 70), the notes were purchased for the Princeton University Library. They were subsequently edited and published as "Walt Whitman's Notes of His Western Trip" in *Biblia*, an occasional publication of the Friends of the Princeton Library, 1 (June 1930): [3]. These jottings record mainly Whitman's Kansas visit, the rail trip to Denver (though nothing of his stay there), and the return stretch through Pennsylvania.

A third base of information is in the over two dozen newspapers of the period reviewed (mainly, but not always, on microfilm) for references to Whitman. Most useful for my narrative are the heretofore uncollected accounts of the jaunt by Whitman's journalist companions: Forney in his Philadelphia weekly, *Progress*, 19 July through 4 October, 1879; Martin in the *Philadelphia Press*, 17 September through 2 October 1879; and Geist in the *Lancaster* (Pennsylvania) *Daily New Era*, 21 July through 25 November, 1879. Geist's report, "The March of Empire—A Fortnight in the Great West," of 1 October 1879, is a good recapitulation of the trip.

Along with these sources I would cite as of special value regarding the Kansas portion of the trip the official account of the Silver Wedding in *The Kansas Memorial, A Report of the Old Settlers' Meeting Held at Bismarck Grove, Kansas, September 15 and 16, 1879*, ed. Charles A. Gleed, 1880. The *Memorial* contains the two-day program, numerous greetings to the convention, the texts of the principal addresses, and a register of about thirty-five hundred Old Settlers. Many of the original documents for the book, including Hale's speech and Whittier's letter regretting his inability to attend, are in the Manuscript Collections of the Kansas State Historical Society at Topeka.

Finally, I wish to acknowledge my debts to Robert R. Hubach, whose scholarship led me a good distance into my subject. Hubach's unpublished Indiana University dissertation of 1943 (available in xerographic form) has a chapter, "Whitman's Trip to the West in 1879," which includes a report of his interview with Linton Usher. The dissertation incorporates Hubach's articles "Walt Whitman in Kansas," *Kansas Historical Quarterly* 10 (May 1941): 150–154; "Three Uncollected St. Louis Interviews of Walt Whitman," *American Literature* 14 (May 1942): 141–147; and "Walt Whitman Visits St. Louis, 1879," *Missouri Historical Review* 37 (July 1943): 386–393. A further report is Hubach's "A Kansas City Newspaper Greets Walt Whitman," *Notes and Queries* (18 December 1943), pp. 365–366. These and his more recent article, "Western Newspaper Accounts of Whitman's 1879 Trip to the West," *Walt Whitman Review* 18 (June 1972): 56–62, cleared the track for me.

Index

121

122

DATE D

PRINTED IN U.S.A.